Madiran and Pacherenc du Vic-Bilh

Premier Wines of South West France

David Mark Perry

ISBN: 978-1495305214
ISBN-: 149530521X

DEDICATION

To Karen and Jon.

CONTENTS

FOREWORD

Madiran, tucked away in France's south west, above the river Adour, is a fascinating part of the wine world. While home to white wines ranging from dry, medium dry to really quite sweet, from the Gros and Petit Manseng and other varieties, it is the red wine, largely and sometimes exclusively from the Tannat grape, which is the most important. This is Madiran. When the wine received its *appellation contrôlée* in 1948, there were said to be 50 hectares in production. Now there are 1500 or so, and the yield is upwards of 70,000 hectolitres a year.

Madiran is an individual wine. It used to be somewhat dense and rustic. Tannat is a late developer, and even with the tendency of the region to enjoy an Indian Summer, was often picked a little too early.

Modern methods and progressive producers have tamed the aggressive tannins. And we now have a wine which is not only unique – nowhere else are there 100 percent Tannat wines – but can be delicious. And prices remain reasonable.

As far as I am aware, this is the first time anyone has dedicated a book exclusively to the wines of this region. David Perry is an *amateur* – a passionate wine lover – in all the best senses of this word. He has produced a splendid guide to the area and its personalities, the producers and their wines. I trust this book will get the success it deserves.

Clive Coates MW 2014

PREFACE

The Oxford English Dictionary traces the root of the word *amateur*, originally a French word adopted by the English, to the Latin *Amator* or lover. This explains my position as a wine writer. This book is a 'labour of love'; I am not a professional critic, a Master of Wine, Sommelier or connected with the wine business in any way. This begs the question, why then write a book on a relatively obscure French wine region?

Firstly I am a lover of the traditional French wine style; I enjoy restrained wines, subtle complexity and wines that have a sense of place. I am fascinated by the concept of *terroir,* the effects of the land and climate on the development of a local identity of artisanal products.

Secondly, I am a Francophile, in particular I love the South West. This is a part of the world steeped in history (and prehistory), predominantly rural with one foot still in a past where people retain their connection to the land. The people are friendly and proud of their heritage; in short *La France Profonde*.

Thirdly, I felt in need of a creative outlet; I have the hands of an artisan, not suited to musicianship, in reality better for digging, planting and other manual tasks. An avid reader, not least of wine books, one in particular was added to my collection by my wife. One Christmas I was given Clive Coates' 'Great Wine Estates of France' in which he describes his favourite producers from across France. Tucked away near the back was a piece on Château Montus and its owner Alain Brumont. I was inspired to taste those wines, along with wines from two others described therein; Domaine Trevallon from Les Baux de Provence and Domaine Huet, a leading estate in Vouvray.

As a wine lover I am fortunate enough to live near Clitheroe in Lancashire, here D Byrne and Co. wine merchants have been plying their trade for over 100 years and unsurprisingly bottles from all three producers were to be found on the shelves along with wines from another of Madiran's top producers, Domaine Berthoumieu. I became a fan of Madiran straight away and sought out further information. It must be said that this presented more of a challenge, as a small *appellation* relatively little has been written about it, with perhaps the most attention paid to the area is a chapter in Paul Strang's excellent 'South West France: The Wines and Winemakers'. I also discovered some French language books on the area which were in a completely different style and some of which were out of date but the seed had been planted.

This book is a personal view of the wines and of the region, I do not profess to be an expert or expect my views to carry the weight of the Jancis Robinsons and Robert Parkers of this world. I have tried to paint a picture of Madiran by finding interesting stories about the leading producers, but not ignoring the smaller wine makers who in turn contribute to the community and show the same craft and commitment to quality.

I have taken time to describe the attributes of the grapes used in the production of Madiran and its white wine counterpart Pacherenc du Vic-Bilh. This is because although the signature grape of Madiran, Tannat, is little known to most wine drinkers, the same can also be said of all the grapes used to make Pacherenc; few people will have heard of Gros and Petit Manseng let alone Petit Courbu or Arrufiac. Some people may have come across the name Tannat due to the recent publicity about the variety's role in determining Madiran as the healthiest red wine in Roger Corder's book 'The Wine Diet'.

I have included information on the different *terroirs* and the way in which they affect the different wine styles along with an explanation of the underlying geology and weather patterns that determine the differences between this region and others on similar latitude. The taming of the tannic Tannat is also of interest given that the process known as micro-oxygenation or *micro-bullage* which is now used all over the world was invented here.

I have also tried to set the area in context with its history, not just the history of wine making but with its connections with the English. As an Englishman I make no apologies for including this chapter as the book is aimed at the English speaking market and I think it provides an interesting historical backdrop. I hope readers will see this book as an aid to discovery of this wonderful area in addition to its wine.

Many wine books include tastings but given the fact I am not a qualified critic as mentioned earlier I think a disclaimer is in order. I have great admiration for the professionals who can taste hundreds of wines in a session and make coherent notes; the vast majority of my tastings are from full bottles, shared with my wife on most occasions. Most are consumed at home as part of a Sunday lunch, the odd one in a restaurant and on occasion at a *gîte* whilst on holiday. The point of this is that maintaining objectivity in such circumstances is difficult. Are the tastings subjective? I would have to admit that they are, but hopefully not enough to make them fatally flawed. My desire is to share an enthusiasm with you the reader, rather than give an authoritative score a la Parker et al. In addition you should not read anything into the absence of a particular wine in the tastings, this is because either I could not get hold of a bottle, or haven't got round to trying it yet. There is a problem with having to self-fund the whole project, despite the low prices of many of the wines I would be loath to pour a glass and throw away the rest. There is also a temptation to taste wines before they are at their best; I'm only human!

ACKNOWLEDGEMENTS

I would like to thank a few people for their assistance; generally a big thank you to all the people and wine makers I have spoken to in the region, in particular Alain Bertolussi and his family at Chateau Viella, Francois Laplace and Jerome Labrouche at Chateau d'Aydie and Didier Barré at Domaine Berthoumieu. I would like to thank Clive Coates for writing the Foreword and last but by no means least my wife Karen for.....well everything really!

CHAPTER 1

THE ENGLISH AND THEIR GASCON COLONY

Eleanor of Aquitaine, a woman ahead of her time.

There has long been a connection between England and Gascony, it all started back in 1152 with the marriage of Henry Plantagenet to Eleanor of Aquitaine. Eleanor was a truly remarkable woman, an epithet over-used in our time of hyperbole, this short biography can only sketch the outline of her life's story.

Eleanor had inherited the Duchy of Aquitaine at the age of fifteen on the death of her father William X in 1137, within four months she married Prince Louis the heir to the throne of France. The death of her father was an opportunity for France to get its hands on Aquitaine and although the land would not be part of the kingdom until inherited through Eleanor's first born son her appointed Guardian King Louis VI, Prince Louis' father, was quick to seize the opportunity. However, France was to be frustrated for three hundred years.

A month after the wedding Louis VI died, Eleanor was Queen consort with influence over France and her own land in Aquitaine. Sadly, for France, Louis and Eleanor never produced a son. The relationship lasted fifteen years and was not without incident. In 1145 Louis was asked to lead the Second Crusade and Eleanor committed her own troops and accompanied the King. It has been suggested that she led her troops into battle dressed as an Amazon, this seems unlikely. The Crusade was a failure and her marriage did not long survive it. Family political differences and, one senses, Eleanor's dissatisfaction with her husband as a leader, made divorce inevitable. The marriage was annulled in 1152 on the grounds on consanguinity; being too closely related.

Within two months she was married to Henry, ironically a closer relative than Louis. Once again in a very short time her husband had become King, in 1154 Eleanor was queen to Henry II, King of England, Count of Anjou, Duke of Normandy and now Duke of Aquitaine. Henry and Eleanor's kingdom now stretched from England's border with Scotland through the western lands of modern France all the way to the Pyrénées. Eleanor's influence, through her family would extend far further than that. Her daughters made significant strategic marriages, Matilda to the Duke of Saxony and Bavaria, Eleanor to the King of Castile and Joan to the Duke of Toulouse. Eleanor deserved the title of matriarch of Europe. Her political influence cannot be over-estimated; she assisted Henry in running English affairs and took the lead in administering Aquitaine, which at that time stretched as far north as the Loire.

Her position changed dramatically in 1173 when she sided with her sons in unsuccessful rebellion against Henry. The failure of the plot led to Eleanor's imprisonment in England where she remained until Henry's death 1189. Richard, her eldest son became King; however it was Eleanor who ruled as Regent when Richard led the Third Crusade. She received no help from her son John, quite the opposite. John rebelled unsuccessfully against Richard but when he became King on his brother's death in 1199 Eleanor still worked unceasingly in support of her son to keep the kingdom intact. She moved to support John when a revolt erupted in Anjou, but suffering from ill heath she took the veil as a nun at the convent of Fontevraud where she died in 1204. On her death Aquitaine was still loyal to England and would remain so until 1453.

Agincourt and all that.

It was the Hundred Years War that put an end to England's rule over Aquitaine and its other dominions in France. One of the events of this period has embedded itself positively in the English consciousness is the battle of Agincourt in 1415. The events have been immortalised by Shakespeare, historians and novelists.

One of the key figures of the battle was a Gascon, a leading political figure in the French royal court, Charles d'Albret the Constable of France from 1402 to 1411 and from 1413 to 1415. The Constable was the first officer of the crown; technically the post holder would outrank all the nobles and answer only to the King.

Charles was born into a noble Gascon family and like many Gascons before and since he made his way as a soldier. At this time the leading French factions were in a state of virtual civil war. The struggle for control of the Royal court was between the Armagnacs of Gascony and the Burgundians. The two protagonists represented differing ways of life, two opposing cultures. The traditionalist Armagnacs held sway at the turn of the century and their appointees filled the key posts in the Kingdom. Their power was overturned when the Duke of Burgundy's army entered Paris in October 1411. Armagnac troops regained control of the capital in 1413 and Charles was reinstated to the post of constable.

England's King, Henry V took advantage of the chaos in Paris to further his claim to the French throne by attacking Harfleur. The King of France had to act and it was left to his nobles and the Armagnacs to confront Henry's army without the assistance of the Duke of Burgundy. Even without this support the French should have been able to deal a crushing blow to the English, but the battle turned into a rout by the technologically superior, though smaller and exhausted English Army. It is suggested that the nobles paid little or no attention to the orders of Charles and Jean II le Maingre, Marshal of France. Charles, leading the first line of attack was killed.

The longbow became a legend as a result of the carnage it reaped although the first ever recorded death by gunshot is arguably more significant historically. The battle helped legitimise the Lancastrian claim to the English throne and broke the power of the Armagnac faction within the French Court. England's hold over Gascony however would finally be lost in 1453 after the Battle of Castillon.

Henri IV, a Gascon King.

Henri Bourbon was born in Pau on 14th December 1553, although born a Catholic he was brought up as a Protestant. He took up the Protestant cause in the Wars of Religion when he joined the Huguenot army. He proved himself a capable and courageous soldier at Arnay-le Duc in 1570, a battle which gained the Huguenots significant concessions from the French King. Henri became King of Navarre in 1572; being a king did not guarantee safety, especially as a Protestant, in 1576 he narrowly avoided the massacre of St Bartholomew as he slipped out of Paris and joined protestant forces.

By 1584 Henri was heir presumptive to the throne of France but was not recognised as such until 1588 when Henri III sought his help to take Paris after being expelled in the aftermath of having the Duke de Guise murdered. Henri III was himself murdered on 1st August 1589 and Henri Bourbon was now King, however he had to fight to secure his Kingdom. It was his conversion to Catholicism in 1593 that was the turning point and he was crowned King in 1594. He is famously quoted as saying *"Paris vaut bien une messe"*, "Paris is worth a mass". His conversion drove a wedge between him and his ally Queen Elizabeth I who was reportedly disgusted and alarmed by his change of heart. Henri effectively put an end to the Wars of Religion with the Edict of Nantes in 1598. This gave Protestants protection and opened up the road to religious tolerance and secularism in France.

Henri IV became a very active king, eliminating the crown's debts by raising taxes but at the same time set about improving agriculture and commerce. He restricted imports to protect French workers, negotiated commercial treaties, re-organised the army and drained the marshes of the *Saintonge* . He set about major building projects, erecting the Louvre, Hotel de Ville and Place Royal. Importantly he avoided military conflicts by achieving his goals by skilful use of diplomacy and beneficial alliances and treaties.

It is difficult to find a more popular public figure in French history; skilled diplomat, courageous soldier and sympathetic to the needs of the common man, a true Gascon! This popularity did not protect him from assassination in 1610 by a Catholic fanatic; such is life.

D'Artagnan; the truth behind the myth.

The story of the Three Musketeers has been known for generations in Britain from TV and film adaptations of Dumas' romantic novel, some have even read it! Almost everyone's favourite is the young, dashing and impulsive hero, D'Artagnan. Unbeknown to the vast majority is the fact that the much beloved character is based upon a real man from Gascony. His name Charles de Batz-Castelmore whose family home is to be found at Lupiac a few miles east of the Adour river and south of the market town of Vic Fezensac.

The real life story lacks some of the romance and swashbuckling adventure of the fictional character but Charles de Batz was still an interesting and important

character in 17th Century France. He was not a gallant protector of courtly ladies, in fact his love life seems to have been a bit of a disaster and very much secondary to his role as soldier and trusted agent of the king.

As seems to be a recurring theme in the lives of young Gascon men Charles made his way as a soldier. He followed his two older brothers into service entering the Kings guard and in 1645 was enrolled into the prestigious Musketeers until it was disbanded. He then served in the Guardes Francaises until the Musketeers were reformed in 1658; he was appointed as a second lieutenant. He became a trusted agent of Cardinal Mazarin

Statue of Charles de Batz in Auch

and acted as the gaoler of Nicolas Fouquet, one of Mazarin's rivals, arrested on a

4

charge of embezzling money from the King's Treasury. He proved to be a considerate gaoler whilst balancing his loyalty to his employer with compassion for the unfortunate Fouquet. This loyal and discreet service brought him to the attention of Louis XIV who also bestowed favour upon him, making him captain-lieutenant of the Musketeers, a very important role answering only to the King.

He was then appointed Governor of Lille, a position for which he was probably ill suited, he didn't enjoy the politics and wasn't popular with those around him. When the opportunity came to return to soldiering he grasped it with both hands, Louis had been keen to extend and solidify his power in Flanders and the Low Countries after wresting Lille from English control and in 1672 his army invaded Holland. Charles was put in charge of the Company of the Grey Musketeers an honour that was to lead to his death. Whilst leading his men in battle at the siege of Maastricht on 25th June 1673 his career came to a bloody end; he was shot through the throat.

Wellington pays a visit.

As the Napoleonic Wars entered their final phase Napoleon's armies and southern France itself faced threats from the British and Portuguese as they prepared to invade from Spain. In the north the Prussians, Austrians and Russians were bearing down on the Emperor. The noose was tightening as France's veteran soldiers delayed the inevitable whilst popular support for the Emperor dwindled. The Peninsula War in Portugal and Spain had raged across Iberia for over five years, over 300,000 French troops were tied down in Spain as the French fought a guerrilla war with one hand and a more conventional conflict with the other. War on more than one front squeezed the resources and will of the French to breaking point.

Late in 1813 the Duke of Wellington's army (if I was being pedantic that should read; Field Marshal Arthur Wellesley's army) was forcing its way through the low passes of the western Pyrénées into France. This was an offensive of manoeuvre and brutal battles; the first priority was to occupy the high ground of La Rhune. Now a popular tourist destination with its mountain railway, the mountain dominated the hinterland of Bayonne allowing the incumbent to observe an opposing army's movement. The operation was achieved by flanking manoeuvres and a brief but bloody assault. The French, seeing their hold on the summit was untenable, retreated to a defensive line just south of the River Nivelle and awaited Wellington's next move. The French were unable to withstand the resulting assault and Marshal Soult's army was forced to fall back in defence of Bayonne.

Soult knew that he could not allow his army to be pinned down and under constant pressure retreated east towards Orthez. This left Bayonne under siege, the city was to hold out for a further two months until it surrendered on the 27th April 1814. Despite regrouping Soult's army virtually collapsed at Orthez at the end of February. It was now a question of how and when Wellington could pin the French down and destroy them or force their surrender.

Wellington split his forces into three corps to pursue and cut off the French line of retreat. General William Beresford, arriving from Bordeaux formed the left flank, General Rowland Hill had the right flank and Wellington was in charge of the centre. Hill in pursuit surprised Soult at Aire sur l'Adour forcing the French army to retreat south towards Tarbes. Hill moved south through Garlin and Lembeye. On the left flank Beresford's men marched through Nogaro and Plaisance. Wellington's corps moved through Saint Mont to Viella on the 18th March and through the village of Madiran to Maubourguet on the 19th. The pursuit was by no means easy, Wellington's army had to negotiate narrow roads through the hilly countryside whilst dragging their heavy siege artillery and supplies with them.

Soult's army was forced to retreat after a battle at Tarbes and again at Toulouse which Wellington captured on the 12th April. News arrived that day of Napoleon's abdication but Soult, refusing to believe the news, did not surrender until the 17th. The war was over; for a short time.

Pau: from garrison to playground.

One of the most interesting and attractive towns in the region, twenty miles to the south of the Madiran vineyards is Pau. On the northern ridge of the valley of the Gave de Pau it is sandwiched between the Madiran and Jurançon wine growing areas. The river flows south and west from the mountains on its journey from its source at the spectacular Cirque de Gavarnie through Lourdes on its one hundred and ten mile journey to the Adour.

Pau was birthplace of Henri IV of France whose castle stands on a knoll above the valley of the Gave de Pau, adjacent to the warren of narrow streets of the old town. The British discovered Pau and its climate when Wellington left a garrison there in 1814, the British settled in and set about anglicising the town.

In the mid-19th century a Scots doctor, Alexander Taylor, came to Pau to recover from Typhus. He was so impressed by the healing powers of Pau's climate that he wrote a book and an influx of rich British families followed him. Many built large villas and English style gardens, some of which can be visited today. This love affair lasted until Biarritz became the fashionable place to be as the well to do followed Queen Victoria's lead in visiting what had become a fashionable and elegant seaside resort. Victor Hugo was a regular visitor and Alphonse Lamartine, poet and founder of the second republic was impressed by what he believed were the incomparable views of the mountains

Even at the turn of the 20th century Pau was still known for its beneficial climate, 'Bradshaws Continental Railway Guide' of 1913 quoted Pau as being,

"known as a very favourable winter and spring residence for consumptive or nervously affective persons- by many it is preferred to the Riviera because of the dry air, absence of wind, and the quieter life".

The British gentry had introduced tea rooms and a way of life including cricket, fox hunting, horse racing. The first full 18-hole golf course in Continental Europe was laid out here from 1856–1860. Motor sport also found a home here, the first race to be called a *Grand Prix* was held in Pau in 1901 and the street circuit is still in use.

Since 1930, Pau has become a mainstay of the Tour de France, the world's greatest cycle race. It is a regular starting point or finish for classic stages which present the competitors with some of their greatest challenges, the Col du Tourmalet, Col d'Aubisque and Col d'Aspin.

Arguably the highest-profile sporting event to be held in Pau is the Étoiles de Pau, this is one of the top six Three-day Eventing competitions held worldwide, two of which are held in England at Burghley and Badminton. Held in late October each year the event attracts the world's top horses and riders competing in Dressage, Cross-Country and Show Jumping.

The Boulevard des Pyrénées exemplifies the relaxed and verdant nature of Pau, even with the rather ugly apartments built in more recent times. The views of the mountains are spectacular and the exotic gardens are pleasant and shady in the heat of high summer.

CHAPTER 2

GEOGRAPHY, TERROIR AND GRAPES

France vies with Italy for the title of the world's largest producer of wine, the wine growing regions provide us with virtually every style of wine from climates that range from the hot and dry in Provence and Languedoc Roussillon to the cold frosty Northern areas such as Chablis. Each has the potential to produce good or even great wines.

In an attempt to ensure that quality and the wine growing heritage are maintained the French authorities introduced rules and regulations for each area and for a wine to qualify for a stamp of approval the wine maker must stick to them. The top delineation is the *Appellation d'Origine Contrôlée*, or A.O.C. The rules tell the wine makers the grapes they can use, they cover the technicalities of vineyard and winemaking practises such as yields per hectare, planting densities, residual sugar content, alcohol levels and so on. A bottle

with this on the label should ensure that the contents adhere to the rules but it does not guarantee that the wine is good. For the buyer the maxim is "know your wine maker".

Madiran and Pacherenc du Vic-Bilh wines achieved the status of an A.O.C. in 1948, this was an achievement to celebrate considering that wine making had been kept alive by a very few wine makers and at the time there were only fifty hectares (one hundred and twenty five acres) under vine. The grape varieties permitted under the A.O.C. rules are Tannat, Cabernet Franc, Cabernet Sauvignon and Fer Servadou for Madiran and Gros Manseng, Petit Manseng, Petit Courbu, Arrufiac and the now little used Semillon and Sauvignon Blanc for Pacherenc.

Since the early days of the *appellation* the area around Viella was added, although why it was excluded in the first place is puzzling especially as it is now one of the highest producing areas for both Madiran and Pacherenc. The proportions of the grape varieties that were allowed in the wines have also changed, culminating in the birth of the pure Tannat wines championed by Alain Brumont. Another area that was specifically omitted was Saint Mont in the north; although the wines there are very similar and some independent producers and the local co-operative make Saint Mont, Madiran and Pacherenc, the area had to wait until 2011 for its own A.O.C. recognition.

Location.

The Madiran area is to be found in the Aquitaine area, tucked up against the valley of River Adour where it ends its progress north and sweeps westwards before turning south west to reach the sea at Bayonne. The vineyards sit astride the intersection of three *departements,* Gers, Pyrénées-Atlantique, and Hautes-Pyrénées; the term *Vic Bilh* translates as 'old country' in the Béarnaise dialect and traditionally refers to the southern part of the wine area, the name Pacherenc refers to the posts supporting the vines. There are no major towns here; Madiran, Viella, Castelnau-Rivière-Basse, Lembeye and Maumusson-Laguian are no more than villages with around five hundred inhabitants each. The other wine villages are little more than hamlets. To the north of the *appellation* Aire-Sur-l'Adour is a larger town and Pau and Tarbes lie to the south, all are outside the A.O.C. limits.

It would be wrong to say that the area is dominated by vines, in fact maize is the major crop with wheat and grazing for cattle also being significant. The vineyards tend to feature on the long slopes and ridges that spread like fingers north westwards from the valley of the Gave de Pau; the soils are dominated by clays. The lower slopes have alluvial deposits, making them more suitable arable farming. Indeed many wine making families were also farmers, few now retain farm land. Although farming can be less of a financial risk, running both businesses concurrently would be a herculean task, particularly when the harvesting of the maize and grapes coincide.

Geology and *Terroir*.

The wine growing areas of Madiran, Saint Mont, Jurançon, the Côte de Gascogne and Armagnac sit on a geological feature called the Lannemezan Cone. This a layer of *molasse*, made up of sediments washed down from the Pyrénées in the Miocene geological epoch. This was then covered by alluvium of sands and pebbles during the Tertiary era and the numerous small rivers that fan out from the mountains have eaten into the layers to produce a series of asymmetric valleys. The west facing slopes tend to be steeper and therefore less suitable for arable crops, providing some of the most exceptional *terroirs* for the production of top quality wines. Notable examples are to be found at La Tyre and St. Lanne. The vines are often to be found alongside areas of woodland and many believe that the trees assist the wine making process by filtering out pollutants in the water supply that the vines rely upon. The east facing slopes have a more gentle gradient and contain a range of *terroirs;* the higher slopes suit the production of traditional and 'high end' Madirans and the lower slopes generally suit fruitier Madiran and both the sweet and dry Pacherencs.

The different *terroirs* to be found in Madiran help determine the style of wine produced from the vines planted on them. Not all wines come from a single *terroir*, individual grape varieties are often planted separately on different *terroirs*, hence blended wines will often, but not always have two or more sites of origin. There are four main types of soil which can be summed up by these examples from land owned throughout the *appellation*, by the Laplace family of Château d'Aydie .

Clays with large pebbles, referred to locally as *argilo-galets*, at Moncaup. Found on the crown of the hills the pebbles catch the sun and warm the soil. This encourages ripening of the fruit and helps with drainage.

Clay with limestone outcrops or *argileaux-calcaire*, for example at the Aydie vineyard at St.Lanne. These soils, especially on this elevated site produce rich, complex wines.

Clay with gravels and quartz sands, found adjacent to the Château at Aydie and at Madiran. These are good for ripe fruity wines.

Lighter wines are made from vines situated on alluvial soils known as *boulbenes* found on the lower slopes sometimes in conjunction with iron and manganese concretions known locally as 'grepp'. 'Grepp' soils are highly sought after here and in other wine areas such as the Médoc in Bordeaux.

However it is not just the soil type that is the issue, the height of the vineyard can affect the temperature, as can the exposure of the slopes; south facing is often seen as the optimum. The relative steepness of a slope can affect the amount of sun the grapes receive as can the orientation of the rows of vines. Some wine makers insist on all the rows of vines being aligned in the same direction, others may be more interested in the slope and its effect on the ability to machine harvest.

Weather and Climate.

The soil and geology are only a part of the story, the element in the whole process that the wine maker can exert little or no control over is the weather. The grape varieties grown in the area have been selected to suit the local climate. The winters can be cold but the spring, although sometimes wet, is not usually prone to damaging late frosts. In turn the summers are warm but although temperatures can be very high for short periods there are not the months of hot weather experienced in Languedoc Roussillon and Tuscany which are both on the same latitude as the *Vic-bilh*. The climate here is moderated by the Atlantic weather system, the coast being roughly fifty miles to the west. The other two areas are very much in the Mediterranean zone with significantly longer periods of heat. This, in addition to the *appellation* specified grape varieties tends to rule out the production of ultra-high alcohol, fruit driven wines.

The long, warm and usually dry autumn is ideal for the ripening of Tannat and Cabernet Sauvignon as well as the later ripening Manseng grapes which are used for the production of Pacherenc. This extended autumn is precipitated by what is known as a *foehn* wind. The winds blow north from the hot Spanish plains, hit the Pyrénées and any moisture falls on the mountains. The residual warm currents flow down the northern slopes and over the south west. This enables grape to be left outside to dry after picking, or to be left on the vine, for what is known as *passerillage,* to concentrate flavours and sugars prior to the crushing and fermentation stage in the winery or *chai*.

Weather can still be a frustration and in some cases it can be disastrous, hail in particular is feared, a storm can destroy a vineyard. In May 2012 Château Montus was devastated by hail when young shoots on hundreds of vines were destroyed in minutes. Similar damage occurred in Burgundy and in Vouvray in June 2013, costing wine makers hundreds of thousands of euros.

Madiran: traditional and modern.

If I had been writing this book twenty years ago I would have used words such as rustic, unyielding and harsh, I would have been describing tannic monsters. Good wines were being made but many were likely to be for those who enjoyed their tannins fierce and appreciated robust, masculine wines that required long ageing. Fortunately the wines being made today are more refined, more complex and have found their place in the world wine market, albeit at the moment, a niche one.

Most makers will produce at least two types of Madiran. The *Tradition*, as the name suggests is the traditional wine style since replaced by special *cuvées* for the signature wine of most *domaines*. A *Tradition* has 60% or more Tannat in the blend with one, two or all three of the other varieties used. The other style is the *Haut de Gamme* or top of the range wine. Many *vignerons* will make this from pure Tannat or with upwards of 80% Tannat, proportions will vary from year to year depending on the quality of the harvest and decisions made during the wine making process. Alain Brumont, by far the largest independent producer has four 100% Tannat *cuvées*. Some of these *cuvées* are only made when the conditions are perfect. A third type is now being made, a 'wine bar', early maturing Madiran, emphasising fruit and easy drinking.

Some *vins de pays* reds, whites and even roses are made. These are blends or varietal wines that do not conform to the A.O.C. regulations, however they can be very serious, quality wines and also very good value for money.

So what can the consumer expect from a Madiran. If you are searching for a new world style 'fruit bomb' look elsewhere. I am yet to find such a wine from the region although one or two of the 'wine bar' style wines are making a nod in that direction. If you are a Pinot Noir aficionado and like nothing more than sipping good Burgundy your pickings here are going to be very thin. The one wine that may interest you is not a Madiran but a *vin de pays* made by Alain Brumont from Pinot Noir with just a little (two or three per cent) Tannat.

Madiran, whether *haut de gamme* or the *Tradition* style, is a food wine, and not food from your local vegetarian tofu bar, it requires meat, usually red and in generous portions. You should expect a comforting, sometimes earthy aroma with red and black fruits. Some wines, with age, will add spice to that along with wood and vanilla from oak, although by no means all wines are aged in oak or rely on new oak to impart flavour and complexity. Flavours are of blackcurrants, damsons, prunes, blackberries, liquorice, some red fruits depending on the *terroir,* the blend and the style. Usually the more Cabernet Franc or Fer Servadou, the more red fruit aromas and flavours will be present. At their very best they can be complex, long with a good balance of fruit and structure.

Tannin is always part of the agenda with Madiran wines; in their youth some wines are quite closed with hard tannins, only revealing hints of future flavours. When mature the tannins soften and in the best wines they become silky and refined. The top wines tend to be medium to medium-full bodied and are made using a minimum of filtration and fining. Sediments are common place so decanting is recommended. I always decant, sometimes for a long time, to allow the wines aromas and flavours to open out. Alcohol levels are by no means high, usually around 13%.

In the last few years a new type of Madiran has emerged and I refer to some of these in my notes as 'wine bar' Madiran. These tend to be simpler, fruity, accessible wines aimed at a younger market. Examples are Tempo from Château Peyros, Joris from Château Laffitte-Teston and Prenium from Cave de Crouseilles.

In his excellent 'The New France: A complete guide to contemporary French wine' Andrew Jefford summed up the taste of Madiran wine perfectly:

"If you could taste a winter night, this is what it would taste like. Smoke from fires, the blackness of cloudy night skies, fruits as shocking as the north wind, tannins with the power of storm-torn earth…."

Madiran: grape varieties.

Tannat is the signature grape that gives Madiran its character; its pre-eminence is enshrined in the A.O.C. regulations and in the hearts of the locals. It is almost certainly a local variety with the first written evidence of it in 1783. The name is probable derived from the word *tanat* which is 'tan coloured' in the Béarnaise dialect. Further evidence of its local origin is the genetic similarity to the local Courbu family of grape varieties.

The vine is vigorous and its growth needs to be controlled to produce quality wines. Many growers achieve this by restricting growth by means of the *guyot simple* method of pruning, where a single fruiting stem is selected and any others removed. In addition some wine makers green harvest, removing bunches of grapes at an early stage, and carry out leaf thinning to aid ripening. High density planting is also used and of course selection of the best *terroirs* is especially important.

Tannat is late ripening which makes it ideally suited to this area which tends to have a stable, warm extended late summer and autumn. The autumn *foehn* winds from the Pyrénées keeps the area dry and warm usually ending the risk of storms and hail.

The smallness of the individual fruits and the thick skins give a clue to its tannic nature. The tradition of Tannat producing harsh tannic wines has been tempered by improved wine making and vineyard practices. For many oak has important role in the wine making process, wines were usually aged in *foudres,* large wooden vats, now the introduction of micro-oxygenation aids the maturing of wines in smaller oak *barriques* and in steel vats.

Most people will have been unaware of this grape variety but it is widespread in the South West of France. It is also a major component of Saint Mont, Tursan, Béarn and Irouléguy wines, all household names to the devotees of the more obscure French wines. A small amount of Tannat vines are also found in Cahors and in other *appellations* but it is unquestionably in Madiran where it produces the best wines.

Tannat has found a second home in an unlikely place, Uruguay, where it represents nearly a quarter of the area under vines. It was imported by settlers from France and has become the country's signature variety. The climate and soils here soften the tannins to produce an easier drinking style, often blended with Merlot and more intriguingly with Pinot Noir.

Cabernet Franc is another local grape variety. More specifically it has been traced to the Spanish Basque country from where it spread north through France. In the Madiran area it is sometimes referred to as Bouchy and used to soften the effects of Tannat's tannic nature. Anyone who has tasted Loire reds will know that Cabernet Franc is capable of producing fruity, aromatic wines. Here it is the only variety contrasting in nature to Tannat and adds aromas and flavours of red fruits.

Cabernet Sauvignon is a *Bordelais* grape and another late ripening variety; it has a thick skin which helps gives wines structure and a potential for ageing. Like Tannat it is high in tannins and in acidity therefore in the context of blending with Tannat ripeness is very important. Along with structure it also contributes aromas of blackcurrant and cedar wood.

The final grape variety allowed in the production of Madiran is **Fer Servadou**. Often referred to simply as Fer or Pinenc it is another variety from the Basque country. Fer means wild or savage and it is another tannic grape that can be challenging for the wine maker. As its name suggests it is often regarded as an unsophisticated or rustic variety, however when it achieves its full ripeness it can add aromas and flavours of red fruits to the blend. Some wine makers are great advocates of the grape whilst others have none in their vineyards. The home of Fer is in the Marcillac *appellation* in Aveyron where it must make up at least 90% of the blend; there it is known as Mansois. It is also found elsewhere in South West France in varying quantities.

Pacherenc du Vic-Bilh: under the wine radar.

If Madiran has been regarded as an obscure wine, Pacherenc du Vic-Bilh has been virtually invisible. This is a great shame as the both the dry and sweet Pacherencs provide a wonderful alternative to more famous and very much more expensive French whites.

The wines were first exported under the Béarnaise name, the name Pacherenc first appeared in the 19th century. These white wines were very important to the area, especially in the west of the region, however their popularity waned and now they represent a small percentage of the wines produced.

The dry or *sec* Pacherencs are often full of exotic tropical fruit, grapefruit, melon and honey, have good underlying minerality with a good lemony acidity. Despite having a rich texture Pacherenc *sec* retains a freshness and balance, which in my humble opinion, is often missing in new world whites. The wines are excellent with fish, pasta and when carefully matched, with white meats. There are very few available in the UK but those that you do find are among the best produced.

The sweet wines come in two styles; the lighter *doux* style is more traditional and akin to Jurançon, gently sweet and can be enjoyed as an *aperitif* or with food. The much richer and sweeter wines are becoming ever more popular; these *moelleux* wines tend to be made with a high proportion of Petit Manseng and are more like Sauternes in style, though not usually in price. One can expect flavours of apricots, oranges, butterscotch, brioche and even truffle in well-aged examples. The sweet wines do not rely on botrytis as do Sauternes, but rather the natural ability of the grape varieties to concentrate the sugars. In some cases grapes are left to dry in the sun after picking, a process referred to as *passerillage*. Wines can now be labelled *vendange tardives*, late harvested, which gives another clue to the level of sweetness; in some years some grapes are harvested as late as December.

Other white wines are marketed as *vin de pays*, often using non A.O.C. sanctioned varieties blended with the local grapes; Alain Brumont even makes a Chardonnay.

Pacherenc: grape varieties.

Petit Manseng is becoming increasingly important in the vineyards. It buds early and produces small fruit that ripens earlier than its derivative Gros Manseng. Early budding can leave it vulnerable to frost damage but this is less of a problem here than in much of France. The skin is thick and the variety has an amazing ability to concentrate sugars, making it ideal in the production of high quality and complex sweet wine. It is also robust enough to lend itself to ageing in oak, a style that is becoming more and more popular. It also manages to balance this richness with a zip of acidity which prevents the wine from becoming cloying. There are those who prefer the lighter sweet wines, the best advice is to try both and make your choice.

Gros Manseng hails from Jurançon, twenty five miles or so to the south like its relative Petit Manseng. It buds early but is late ripening which makes it ideally suited to a region with low risk of frost and a long warm late summer and autumn. Its thick skin is not prone to botrytis and its high sugar content is matched with high acidity. Its tendency to be relatively late ripening makes it less able to be used in the making of really sweet wines so its importance is in decline. However it is used to good effect in the dry whites and *doux* wines.

Another variety from Jurançon is **Petit Courbu**. This variety has small bunches of small fruits that are susceptible to Botrytis and hence tends to be picked early. It is used for dry wines where it is valued for its freshness and aromatics, but using this variety with oak, particularly new oak requires skillful handling. It brings lovely lemon, lime and grapefruit flavours with good minerality and elegance. Some *vignerons* make a single varietal wine from Petit Courbu though its early ripening can throw the cycle of the vineyard into confusion particularly when used as part of a blend; perhaps this explains the relative rarity of the practice. This is a shame as there are wonderful examples of Pacherencs made with Petit Courbu.

Arrufiac or Arrufiat as it is sometimes referred, has shown signs of decline in recent years. A relative of Petit Courbu it is late ripening with large bunches of large fruits. It can be susceptible to mildew and is not suited to making the very sweet style of wine. It has declined in importance though some Pacherencs are still made with it. It may have disappeared altogether had André Dubosc of Producteurs Plaimont not led the movement to save it from obscurity.

Sauvignon Blanc and **Semillon** can also be used but I have yet to find a wine other than *vin de pays* that include their use.

It's all about *terroir*. Stony ground at La Tyre vineyard.

CHAPTER 3

WINE MAKING IN THE VIC-BILH

History

Although there is evidence that wines were being made in the region in Gallo-Roman times the evidence of vines being planted in the modern day *appellation* begins with the founding of a Benedictine priory in Madiran in the year 1030. The first written evidence is from the 13th century archives which record that vines were being grown throughout the area and that the production of wine was a valuable addition to the economy. The church belonging to the Priory still stands, the site also houses Le Prieure, a high quality restaurant and hotel and the Maison des Vins.

At this time the trade was undoubtedly localised, in the 15th century the evidence suggests that the major markets were the towns of the Bigorre area and further south towards the Pyrénées. This is not surprising considering the valley of the river Adour and the river itself formed a natural highway along which the wine barrels could be transported, this remained the major trade route until the 19th century which saw great improvements in the transport infrastructure.

By the 16th century the vines are known to have been grown in rows, as they are today, this is notable as it would have been seen as a sign of quality. It wasn't just money that changed hands, the wine makers accepted goods for their wine. Wood and building stones were traded, evidence of this can still be seen in the old farm houses and wine producers buildings. Ironically trade with Britain included the import of maize, which was in short supply.

Ripe Tannat grapes at Château Pichard

The 17th century saw another market opening up for the red wines; the French founded colonies in the West Indies in the first half of the century, French Guiana in 1624, a year later St Kitts and Martinique with Guadeloupe following in 1635. The wines were shipped to the West Indies from Bayonne, having been floated there on the Adour or carted down the valley. The tannic nature of the wine was of benefit in this case as wines needed to be robust if they were to withstand the long journey and the high temperatures at the destination.

By the 18th century the wines were being sold under the name Madiran, the first mention of the name is found in 1744. The wine was now the dominant money maker in the region although the rearing of cattle and the growing of wheat and maize were becoming significant. The 18th century also saw the development of markets for the sweet white wines particularly in Holland where similar wines from Jurançon, Monbazillac and Sauternes were gaining in popularity. The grape varieties of Cabernet Sauvignon, Fer Servadou and of course Tannat were also now being mentioned by name.

However there was a shadow on the horizon, a blight that was to all but destroy the wine trade in Europe, *Phylloxera*. *Phylloxera Vastatrix* as it was known or *Daktulosphaira vitifoliae,* is an aphid that arrived in France half way through the 19th century, the damage it caused was catastrophic. Whole vineyards failed as toxins injected into the vines as the aphid fed, destroyed the root system of the plants. In thirty years the wine industry shrank by nearly half causing widespread job losses and wage cuts. In some ways the Madiran area actually benefitted from the woes of the rest of France, the problem arrived late in the South West, by which time a strategy had been put in place to deal with the disaster. At the turn of the century the area was still achieving record production whilst at the same time massive replanting of new rootstocks was put in place. This was an expensive venture and many small wine makers, peasant farmers, could not afford the expenditure and looked for other ways to survive. Maize production started to increase at the expense of vines and many poor quality rootstocks failed.

The first half of the 20th century was not kind to Madiran wines, two world wars, an economic depression and the echoes of the *Phylloxera* crisis, saw massive decreases in the area under vine. Maize production became, and remained the mainstay of the region and the names Madiran and Pacherenc looked likely to be consigned to history. Few wine makers persisted with only fifty hectares being under vine at the end of the Second World War.

It would be a reasonable assumption that the areas promotion to an *Appellation d'Origine Contrôlée,* in 1948, would be the kick start that the area needed. However it was only a partial success. The original regulations imposed on the wine makers were undoubtedly an attempt to put in place processes that would help to tame the tannic nature of the wines but they were restrictive and more importantly very expensive to implement. The insistence on long periods, nearly three years, of barrel ageing would put a huge financial burden on small scale producers for both the capital outlay required and the restricted cash flow. The only answer was the development of co-operatives; they played a major part in the survival of the new *appellation*. It made much better economic sense for the small scale grower to sell their grapes to the co-op and spread the financial risk rather than make their own wine. Little wonder that at this time there were only six producers looking to go it alone.

As the regulations of the A.O.C. relaxed and the area expanded a new generation of wine makers arrived who looked to make their own wines. The area of land under vine increased, by 1970 there were over 120 hectares. The 1980's saw that figure rise to over 700 hectares and at by 1990 the area was edging towards the thousand mark. Now the figure is over 1 500, over 1 300 hectares for Madiran and just under 200 hectares for Pacherenc. However, even when the area under vines for the making of non-appellation wines is added this total is only approximately a third of the area under vine at the end of the 19th century. Despite the increase in size the area is still small, Bordeaux *appellations* cover an area nearly one hundred times the size and Burgundy is nearly twenty times greater in size. Although Madiran wine is more akin to Bordeaux the industry here bears more resemblance to Burgundy, with small family holdings rather than wine making being dominated by Châteaux owned by multi-national corporations found in the top estates of Bordeaux.

The growth in area under vine in the second half of the 20th century has been mirrored by the growing number of independent wine makers; by the late sixties there were a dozen independents bottling their own wine, by the end of the 1970's a new generation had taken that to twenty-one and now there are over fifty independent wine makers. The majority make both Madiran and Pacherenc. With the increase in independents so the need for better organisation and marketing arose, the drives to improve quality and develop new markets have led to the constitution of bodies such as the romantically named *'Mousquetaires du Madiran'* instigated by the then owner of Domaine Tailleurguet, André Dartigues in the 1970's to the modern day, internet friendly, *Altema* and other groups involving both the co-operatives and independents. The shrinking home market and the need to break into foreign markets has focused minds on the future, not only how to improve the management of marketing and distribution but also on how to respond to new trends. Prohibitive government legislation and the cultural changes being seen throughout France are other challenges facing the industry.

Wine making improvements.

Without doubt there have been huge improvements In wine making practises from vineyard to bottling. The introduction of stainless steel equipment, easy clean materials and good quality machinery and barrels have helped improve the overall standard of wine making and helped reduce the need for additives, not only here but throughout France. Attention to detail and a palpable desire to improve quality have in themselves led to improvements; there is now a 'can do' attitude amongst wine makers and a pride in the wines being made. Pacherenc is a classic example. Although only produced in relatively small quantities, around a fifth of the total wine production, there has been a positive response to changes in the market. Excellent dry Pacherencs are now produced. Changes have been made to respond to the increasing preference for the very sweet, *moelleux* style over the traditional more gently sweet *doux* wines by the planting of more Petit Manseng at the expense of other varieties.

Concerted efforts have been made to seek out and utilise the best *terroirs* and to experiment with different styles of Madiran; from the production of super-*cuvées* to the development of wines for earlier consumption and where food is not necessarily needed as an accompaniment. Major investments have been made by some wine makers to enable the construction of subterranean and temperature controlled cellars, mainly for the ageing of the red wines.

De-stemming and hand picking of grapes, leaf removal and green harvesting are commonplace and all help to produce riper and top quality fruit. Long maceration and gentle treatment of the grapes also reduces unwanted, excess tannins. The new generation of wine makers were the first to study at oenology institutes and gain experience in other *appellations*, a trend that continues. The result is a far more professional approach and a better understanding of the processes and a move towards more sustainable vineyard practises.

Micro-oxygenation: where Madiran leads the world follows.

The introduction of steel tanks created its own problems for makers attempting to produce an earlier maturing Madiran. The new techniques were, at first, disastrous. The Madirans produced often became reductive with volatile sulphur compounds being produced. This imparted a smell of rotten eggs and cabbage. Wine with this 'nose' tends not to sell and an alternative had to be found.

It is largely for this reason that the process of micro-oxygenation or *micro-bullage*, was developed in this relative backwater. Patrick Ducournau developed the process in 1991. Basically it is a computer controlled system for adding minute amounts of oxygen into the wine through a *cliquer*. In its simplest form this is a tube with holes in it. The amounts are so small that they are absorbed by the wine before they can break the surface of the liquid. The theory is that these small amounts of oxygen help to improve the structure of the wine, stabilise its colour, reduce the production of reductive elements and smooth the tannins.

Not all Madiran producers use the process, Alain Brumont has developed his own 'racking' system, which is a more traditional approach to wine making. Racking or *soutirage* is the action of moving the liquid from one barrel to another during the ageing period. Others use the process known as *délestage*, where the wine is pumped over the crust of skins that float to the top of the wine.

Micro-oxygenation is used worldwide and although some of the claims made about the effectiveness of the process may be questionable there can be no doubting the influence it has on wine making across the globe.

Healthiest wine.

If the claims made for the benefits of micro-oxygenation attract controversy so does the claim that Madiran is the most healthy red wine. The case is expounded by Professor Roger Corder in his book 'The Wine Diet' first published in 2007. In it he seeks to explain the 'French paradox', in that France has relatively low levels of heart disease despite the high levels saturated fat in the national diet. In Gascony the paradox is even more exaggerated, there are twice the number of men aged ninety or more here than the national average; this in an area renowned for its meats, *foie gras* and hearty meals.

The explanation, he argues, is that wine consumption, in particular of the local Tannat based wines which contain the highest level of procyanidins of any wine, has a beneficial effect on the local population. The compounds are found in the grape pips and the small size of the Tannat grape explains the high proportion of the compound in the juice the it produces. The procyanidins dissolve into the wine during fermentation; this he explains can reduce the risks of heart disease and of cancer. This is a simple synopsis and of course the benefits of Madiran as with any 'wonder' food only work in conjunction with other foods and in the case of alcohol consumption, when taken in moderation. So not a bottle a day!

Vintage Charts.

Madiran	Vintages
Exceptional	2000, 2005, 2009
Excellent	1995, 1998, 1999, 2004, 2008
Very Good	2001, 2002, 2003, 2006, 2007, 2010, 2011
Good	2012, 2013

Pacherenc du Vic-Bilh	Vintages
Exceptional	1996, 2000, 2001, 2005
Excellent	2004, 2009
Very Good	2003

Vintages in the region tend to be reasonably consistent due to the moderate climate. You will notice that there are no years that are regarded as poor, it is extremely rare to have a disastrous year across the whole of the appellation. That is not to say that individual domains may not suffer setbacks, due to hail for example.

There are wines from years on the Madiran chart that will still be at their peak, these are likely to be those with high levels of Tannt. Some of the older vintages of blended wines will have started to fade and lose their fruit flavours.

The chart for Pacherenc refers to sweet wines. Some of the wines from the years listed will still be developing and, as is the nature of sweet wines, could improve for many years to come.

CHAPTER 4

THE ROLE OF THE CO-OPERATIVES

Producteurs Plaimont
Route d'Orthez
32400 Saint-Mont
Gers
Tel: 33 (0)5 62 69 69 50
Website: www.plaimont.com
Open: Monday to Saturday: 9am to 7pm.
Sunday: 10am to 7pm.
Also outlets at Aignan and Plaisance.
2 500 hectares, Saint-Mont, Madiran, Pacherenc, Vins de Pays.
Production: 34 000 000 bottles.

Cave de Crouseilles
64350 Crouseilles
Pyrénées-Atlantiques
Tel: 33 (0)5 59 68 57 14
Email: info@crouseilles.com
Website: www.crouseilles.com
Open: Monday to Saturday: 9am to 1pm and 2pm to 7pm.
Sunday: 10am to 7pm.
587 hectares, Madiran, Pacherenc, Vins de Pays.
Production: 3 000 000 bottles.

The importance of wine co-operatives in France should not be underestimated. They account for over 50% of the total wine production and dominate the *vin de pays* and *vin de table* markets. This dominance in the lower end markets does not mean that quality wines are not produced, rather they enable a large number of growers to make a living, preserve valuable *terroirs* that might otherwise be lost and provide wines at affordable prices. Many growers are unable to afford to make their own wines, others prefer to be simple growers without the stresses involved when competing in an often unpredictable market place.

The fact that virtually all co-operatives (97%) are in rural municipalities is of particular value. Eight thousand jobs, one hundred and ten thousand growers, the production of five hundred million bottles and a turnover of around six billion euros are vital to rural economies. Co-operatives also have the financial clout to place wine in supermarkets, market wine at home and in the export market; for example a large proportion of Madiran and other local wines that find their way to the U.K. are from the Plaimont Group.

Co-operatives play a very important role in the production of Madiran and Pacherenc. **Producteurs Plaimont** and **Cave de Crouseilles**, who joined forces to form the Plaimont Group in 1999, produce approximately 50% of the Madiran and 60% of the Pacherenc made. The Plaimont Group is vital to the local economy, not only within the Madiran *appellation* but also in the wider context of the wine growing areas of Gascony.

Producteurs Plaimont is a remarkable organisation, dynamic and forward looking yet based in a comparatively lowly wine region. Located in Saint-Mont it is almost synonymous with Saint-Mont wines. Saint-Mont until recently was a *VDQS appellation, Vin Delimité de Qualité Supérieure* though in 2011 it upgraded to an *Appellation d'Origine Contrôlée*. The name Plaimont is derived from the villages of Plaisance, Aignan and Saint-Mont whose co-operatives amalgamated in 1979.

The co-operative's growers are scattered across the region and in addition to Saint-Mont, of which they account for 97% of the total production, Madiran and Pacherenc, they also provide grapes for the production of Vin de Pays de Côtes de Gascogne, Béarn and Côtes de Condomois wines. The five thousand hectares of group owned vines produce around forty million bottles. Average holdings are between six and seven hectares, if you do the maths you can see how important the group is to local communities.

Saint-Mont can be of excellent quality, my personal favourites are the red and white, Le Faite wines. They have a distinctive appearance with their wooden tags and waxed tops, I always end up with bits of wax in the glass! In addition the L'Empriente de Saint-Mont white wine is another that has made the eight hundred mile trip home in the boot of my car.

There are a number of Madirans and Pacherencs produced, namely **Plenitude, Arte Benedicte, Maestria, Terres de Moraines,** Maestria, Saint Albert and L'Or du Vieux Pays.

Cave de Crouseilles, in the Madiran *appellation,* has over two hundred growers cultivating over four hundred and fifty hectares of vines. Formed in 1950 it soon became the dominant producer in the area at a time when most growers struggled to make a living in the wine industry. At that time the company provided the best option for many and continues to do so. It provides incomes for the growers, wine makers and administrative and sales staff. The production here is in the region of five million bottles including wines made for the estates of Châteaux d'Arricau Bordès and Mascaràas.

The Co-ops mainstay is a **Tradition** Madiran which is aged for one year in tank with some *élevage* in oak *barriques*. The new more modern style wine, **Prenium**, prepared from grapes harvested from young vines is made for early drinking. Tannat dominated *Grandes Vins* receive a minimum of one year's *élevage* in oak *barriques* using grapes from the best *terroirs*. **Château D'Arricau Bordès** and **Château Mascaràas** are excellent examples.

Pacherencs are made from vines on east to south east facing slopes that catch the morning sun the warm autumn evenings assist the process of *passerillage* late in the growing season. The *vendange* can last well into December a good example of the sweet wines are the being the Château D'Arricau Bordès and Hivernal.

The **Cave Co-operative du Madirannais** seemed to have turned a corner when Alain Brumont offered the services of his wine maker and his *chai* and an outlet known as *Torus* was opened on the main road from Riscle to Tarbes, however the experiment failed to gain momentum and the facility closed.

Vines, woods and mountains.

Tastings:

Chênaie du Tilh 2010, Madiran.
Deep ruby. Cherries, tomato and vanilla oak on the nose. Black fruits and damsons overlain by oaky vanilla. Quite drying but good with red meat.
June 2013

Prenium de Crouseilles 2010, Madiran.
Dark garnet, with aromas of sour cherry and very ripe sweet fruit. Red fruits and liquorice with a layer of sweet vanilla oak on the palette. Modern fruity Madiran.
June 2013

Collection Plaimont, élevé en fûts de chêne 2009, Madiran.
Dark Purple with black fruits and brambles on the nose. Liquorice and black fruit flavours. Tannins still a little rough, has the structure to age . Good value for money.
May 2013

Château de la Motte 2002, Madiran.
Mid garnet. On the nose black fruits but also lots of raspberry and hints of truffle. The palette has depths of black fruit underlain with red fruits. Lovely and elegant, relatively light for Madiran but this has matured wonderfully well. Highly recommended.
January 2014

Château de Mascaràas 2005, Madiran.
Dark garnet. Sweet blackcurrants and liquorice on the nose. Similar on the palette but with hints of prune and lingering red fruits. Not as full as the previous wine but has lasted well. Good
January 2014

Reserve des Tuguets 2010, Plaimont, Madiran.
Medium Ruby. Blackcurrants, red fruits and vanilla on the nose. Black currant and ripe cherry flavours with hints of mocha and liquorice. Solid Madiran but needs food. Available at Tesco.
February 2014

Hivernal 2009, **Pacherenc Moelleux.**
Petit Manseng and a little Gros Manseng
Medium/deep gold. *Confit* oranges, spice and honey on the nose. On the palette oranges, prunes and truffle enrobed in honey. Citrus acidity keeps it fresh. Lovely sweet wine from grapes picked a few days before Christmas.
January 2014

CHAPTER 5

DIDIER BARRÉ, A MADIRAN MUSKETEER.

Domaine Berthoumieu
Didier Barré
32400 Viella
Gers
Tel: +33 (0)5 62 69 74 05
Email: barre.didier@wanadoo.fr
Website: www.domaine-berthoumieu.com
Open: Monday to Saturday: 8am to 12pm, 2pm to 6pm.
Sunday and bank holidays by appointment.
26 hectares, Madiran, Pacherenc and Vins de Pays.
Production: 180 000 bottles.

Didier Barré is without doubt one of the leading wine makers in the appellation for both his Madirans and his Pacherencs. I have to admit that he is probably my favourite wine maker, due to the wines he makes and the charm and pride he exudes when you meet him to talk about his work. He is an enthusiastic and welcoming host, when we arrived for our first visit to the *domaine* he was disappearing down a track to his vines, but when he saw us he jumped down from his tractor and trotted over to introduce himself. On my last visit during the 2013 *vendange* Didier waved goodbye from his tractor as he moved from vineyard to vineyard to ensure everything was running smoothly.

I enjoy a wine tasting that little bit more when the *vigneron* samples the wine with me. Didier has the quirk of emptying a few millilitres of wine, from the newly opened bottle, into the spittoon before ensuring it is fit to taste. His enthusiasm is evident as he explains the work that goes in to producing each wine.

The estate, dating back to 1850, has been in the family for six generations. Didier's grandfather and uncle were local *negociants;* Didier was more interested in wine making and the future of the family *domaine*. In 1980 he travelled to Burgundy to study and in 1983 returned to work with his father. He took over the running of the business and wine making in 1995. By this time he had already introduced the **Cuvée Charles de Batz** using the oldest vines. His intention was to produce a wine that would be full and rich but having finesse and elegance; not a common trait in Madiran at that time. In 2000 he created a *super-cuvée*, **Argelys**, from one hundred year old Tannat vines, his aim to produce a wine that has exceptional sweetness for a Madiran.

Didier's faith in the Tannat grape reflects that of Alain Brumont and he is happy to acknowledge the debt owed to the icon of Madiran wines. He told me:

"I am one of a generation of wine makers who have followed in the footsteps of Alain Brumont in developing an understanding of the importance and nobility of the Tannat grape".

There are twenty-six hectares of vines. As is the norm in the *appellation* the majority, twenty-one hectares, are for Madiran with three and a half hectares for Pacherenc and the remainder for *vins de pays*.

There are two types of soils in the vineyard, on the plateau there is clay with pebbles or *galets*. Here the soil heats up quickly and produce smooth, complex, age worthy wines. The other

Labels for the 2010 vintage of Berthoumieu's Charles de Batz on the machine and ready to roll

terroir is on the slopes and contains clay and gravel loam, more suited to early maturing fruity wine. The vines range from ten to one hundred years of age.

During the winter months the vines are pruned to a single, one year old branch, known as a *guyot simple.* This branch will bear the buds for the next year's fruit, this enables Didier to reduce yields and improve quality. In spring any dead vines are replaced; in addition when the buds appear any that are surplus to requirements are removed and those remaining are trained to grow upwards. This helps to gain maximum benefit from the sun's rays to encourage full ripening.

In summer like many other growers, Didier removes a proportion of the leaf growth to improve the prospects for well ripened fruit. This is especially important for tannic grape varieties like Tannat and Cabernet Sauvignon. In addition Didier carries out a green harvest, reducing the number of bunches on the vine. The long warm late summer and autumn is vital in the development of ripe fruit especially when the vines used here are late ripening varieties. Wine makers test the acidity of the grapes regularly to determine the best time to harvest; this varies with the type of wine that is being made.

Didier is a great believer in strengthening the vine to enable it to resist disease rather than rely on chemicals to cure problems. To do this he uses TonyX treatments; these are preparations of trace elements that are provided in blocks or powders. He is committed to improving the vineyards and uses PRP Technologies additives to help with the chemical, biological and structural health of the soil. The aim is to support biodiversity and biological activity, prevent soil erosion, compaction and reduce the incidence of mineral lock out and leaching of nutrients from the soil.

Didier is at the forefront of local producers in their efforts to promote the areas wines. In 1996 he joined forces with wine makers from across the south west in setting up the organisation 'Expressions de Terroir'. This group not only promotes their products but also sells them across the globe. The administrative offices are in Valence d'Agen and from there the orders are transferred to the company Fleurons de Lomagne who handle all the logistics.

As mentioned above there is a *super-cuvée*, **Argelys**, made with grapes from the oldest Tannat vines; it doesn't bear the *domaine* name only that of Monsieur Barré himself. Price ££££

Didier's *Haut de Gamme* is the excellent **Cuvée Charles De Batz**. In most vintages there is upwards of 90% Tannat, with the balance made up of Cabernet Sauvignon. The vines average over fifty years of age and the yield is limited to 40hl per hectare. The Tannat is fermented and macerated for thirty days, the Cabernet Sauvignon for twenty. The must receives *pigeage* or pressing, on a daily basis. The clear juice of each variety is aged separately in new oak *barriques,* the Tannat for eighteen months and the Cabernet for twelve. The wine is blended and bottled twenty two months after harvest. The wine will age for ten years or more. It is regarded as one of the best made Madirans. Price ££

The third *cuvée* **Haute Tradition** is a blend of 55% Tannat, 35% Cabernet Sauvignon and 10% Fer Servadou. Like virtually all producers the Tradition style is the mainstay of the *domaine*, although the headline making is generally done by the special *cuvées*. The Tannat is fermented and macerated for twenty five days the other grapes for twenty one, again with daily *pigeage*. The juice spends eighteen months in oak *barriques* that are two to four years old and may receive fining with egg whites if it is necessary. Bottling is twenty two

29

months after harvest. This wine will be ready to drink in three to four years but may benefit from more time. Price £

Gaia, Didier's dog, checks the ripeness of the Tannat. She enjoys her work!

The Pacherenc du Vic Bilh Sec is a blend of 50% Gros Manseng, 25% Petit Manseng and 25% Petit Courbu. The vines are on the lower gravel slopes and average over fifty years of age. The yield is limited to 50hl per hectare and grapes are handpicked in one session to preserve the freshness and aromas of the fruit. Didier is a great believer in doing everything to maintain this freshness. The grapes are macerated for twenty four hours and cold stabilised on their lees for a fortnight. Fermentation and ageing is done half in stainless steel and half in new oak *barriques* at between eighteen and twenty degrees. The juice is stirred on its lees bi-weekly to get the best aroma and improve the structure of the wine. Price £.

Symphonie d'Automne is Didier's sweet Pacherenc. This is definitely of the sweeter, *moelleux* style and very highly regarded. It is made from 90% Petit Manseng and 10% Petit Courbu. The vines, on the gravel slopes, average over fifty years of age and the yields are 30hl per hectare. The grapes are handpicked over three *'tries'* or passes, through the vineyard in November and December. This ensures that only the fruit that is perfect is used and that the aromas of *confit* fruits and honey are preserved. Fermentation and ageing is carried out in new oak *barriques*. The wine will age for ten years or more but the purity of the fruit also makes it enjoyable to drink young. Like Jurançon wines the sweetness is matched with a freshness that stops them becoming heavy or cloying. Price £

Didier Barré was the first *vigneron* to produce and market a *vin de liqueur*, inspired by one of his friends in the Douro. **Tanatis** is made from very ripe Tannat grapes whose fermentation is halted by the addition of neutrally flavoured alcohol. Port like, rich and fruity it can be enjoyed as an *apéritif* or a *digestif*. Price ££.

Tastings:

Argelys 2009, Madiran.
100% Tannat.
Deep Purple colour, very glossy. Pencil shavings, hedgerow and prune sweetness on the nose. Creamy prunes with blackcurrants dominating the long finish. Possibly a little disjointed at present, it needs time to develop and fulfil its potential. Good now, I expect this to be very, very good. I need to hide the 2010!
December 2013

Cuvée Charles de Batz 2006, Madiran.
90% Tannat and 10 % Cabernet Sauvignon in this vintage.
Deep ruby colour, very glossy. On the nose, pencil shavings and good ripe blackberry fruit. On the palette, liquorice and lingering blackcurrant and bramble flavours. A little bitter edge on the finish. Good length.
This is a good example of a top Madiran, masculine but well made. This wine may improve with more ageing. Excellent.
January 2012

Another bottle 7 months on.
Further evolved; the tannins smooth and less evidence of any bitterness. Lovely fruit. Delicious.
August 2012

Haute Tradition 2008, Madiran.
55% Tannat, 35% Cabernet Sauvignon, 10% Fer Servadou.
Deep garnet. Aromas of red fruits and liquorice. More mineral than the **Charles de Batz**, red fruits with a touch of liquorice on the finish. A little vegetal in the middle palette. Good food wine, good acidity but lacks a little fruit. Great value.
October 2012

Vielle Vignes 2010, **Pacherenc Sec.**
50% Gros Manseng, 25% Petit Manseng and 25% Petit Courbu.
Straw yellow colour with apricots and honey on the nose. White peaches and peach stones on the palette, floral notes on the finish. Nicely balanced acidity.
July 2013

Symphonie D'Automne 2008, **Pacherenc Moelleux.**
100% Petit Manseng.
Deep amber in colour with aromas of butterscotch and *confit* orange. Flavours of *confit* orange, jammy apricots with a layer of refreshing citrus fruit. Long and good depth with the potential to improve further. One of the very best.
June 2013

CHAPTER 6

CHÂTEAU D'AYDIE, A GLOBAL INFLUENCE IN MODERN WINE MAKING

Château d'Aydie
Famille Laplace
64330 Aydie
Tel: 05 59 04 08 00
Email: contact@famillelaplace.com
Website: www.famillelaplace.com
Open: Monday to Saturday 9am to 12.30pm and 2pm to7pm.
Sunday by appointment.
60 hectares, Madiran, Pacherenc and Vins de Pays.
Production: 600 000 bottles.

The Laplace family is arguably the most influential in Madiran both for their long term commitment to the region and their contribution to the world of winemaking in general. The full range of wines is held in high regard and the Pacherenc sec, Cuvée Frederic Laplace is certainly a contender for 'best in *appellation*'. Beautifully made, elegant and full of fruit it sets a benchmark for other makers to follow.

The *domaine*, or to be more accurate *domaines,* make up one of the largest estates in the *appellation*. The family manage Chateau d'Aydie along with Domaine Mouréou and Chapelle Lenclos. Aydie is the original family property, the other smaller *domaines* are owned by a cousin of the Laplace family, Patrick Ducournau. The estates are run by Bernard, Francois, Jean-Luc and Marie Laplace.

The siblings are the third generation to have a significant effect on the *domaine* and the *appellation*. The family was instrumental in saving Madiran as a wine growing area. In the 1930's the estate was small with only six hectares under vine, the other land was agricultural. Frederick Laplace, grandfather to the current generation, began bottling his own wine and was determined to preserve the areas wine making heritage, a hugely significant contribution in the context of a total area under vine of approximately fifty hectares at the time the *appellation* status was granted in 1948. His son Pierre was one of, if not the first, *vigneron* to recognise the importance of the Tannat grape to Madiran. He set about identifying *terroirs* that would bring out the best in it.

In the first half of the 20th century white wines were far more significant to producers incomes than they are today, particularly in the west of the region. The Laplace family have maintained a commitment to producing white wines, with an emphasis on the use of Petit Manseng. They are renowned for their high quality Pacherencs.

As the appellation grew in size so did the Laplace family holdings. The Château d'Aydie, across the road from the original family farm is surrounded by vines and has splendid views of the Pyrenees. It has a modern *Chais* with 400 litre *barriques*; the original *foudres* are on show in the tasting room. However in April 2010 the property was minutes from being the scene of a tragedy when an electrical fault caused the roof to catch fire. Francois and his family live in the building and it was his son who raised the alarm enabling Francois' wife and daughter to escape the blaze. Francois, who was out early that morning, returned to find the roof engulfed in flames. Thirty fire fighters with four engines managed to get the fire under control, limiting the damage and preventing the fire spreading to the cellars.

The author surveys the vines at Château d'Aydie

In addition to the thirty-five hectares held under the name of Château d'Aydie there are another fifteen at Domaine Mouréou and Chapelle Lenclos, in Maumusson-Languian. The management arrangement enables their cousin Patrick Ducourneau to continue with his research and advisory work. His current project is an 'oak chip' business, providing the chips to wine makers to add to their wine, this is not legal everywhere but is big business nevertheless.

The Laplace holdings are spread throughout the region, over the years the family have sought out land with some of the best *terroirs*. The vineyards the Château and the village of Madiran are on clays mixed with gravels and quartz sands. The vines on the steeper slopes of La Tyre at *Saint Lanne* are on clays with limestone and produce some of the most complex and rich wines of the *appellation*. Further to the south at Moncaup the high slopes are warm and well drained. There are vines at Lascazères, Conchez-de-Béarn and Vialer and on the lower slopes near the Château where the vines are sited on richer alluvial soils that produce soft fruity *vin de pays* wines.

By most definitions the Laplace family are relatively small producers however their influence on global wine production has been enormous; the reason being that the process of micro-oxygenation, locally known as *micro-bullage* was invented and developed here. The process, which allows tiny amounts of oxygen to be added to the wine, was the brainchild of Patrick Ducourneau. It was originally developed in an attempt to tame the tannic nature of the Tannat grape, however it is used worldwide to soften wines. It is not without its critics and there have been research reports both supporting and undermining the claims made for its benefits. Francois explained that the process was not used to speed up the ageing process. Wine maker Jerome Labrouche elaborated, explaining that micro-oxygenation allowed them to make the tannins more rounded and better integrated into the wine. It is used at the end of the fermentation period when the colour and taste of the must are checked, if the tannins are 'green' the process is implemented. It is not used on all wines or in every vintage, in 2011 for example, the conditions in the vineyard were good and as Jerome explained "nature did a good job that year and we did as little as possible to the wine".

Jerome shows the author a 'cliquer'

Jerome was brought in as winemaker in 2010, a sign of change at Aydie. Although a local, he is from Aire-sur-l'Adour, over the border in the Landes *departement*. he is well travelled. He has worked in St. Estephe, the USA and at the De Lucca winery near Montevideo in Uruguay. He explained that the Tannat from Uruguay was producing very different wines due to the sandy soils and blending with grape varieties not permitted in the Madiran *appellation*. His job at Château d'Aydie is to present alternatives to the family and work closely with Bernard and Francois in the vineyard and the *Chai*. He explained that the vintages tend to be very consistent here due to the climate and the attention to detail in the vineyard. Leaf removal takes place early in the year and green harvesting is carried out in August. The harvest is completed in November; Jerome explained that there was a risk of botrytis in some areas of the vineyard which is unusual here, but it can help to increase the concentration of fruit flavours. The 2013 *vendange* at Aydie, Jerome explained was definitely a good one although due to the heavy rains in spring and early summer it was better suited to the production of fruity wines rather than classic Madiran.

The *Chai* is equipped with an antique micro-oxygenation system, not one of the shiny new ones, but the techniques and rest of the equipment are modern. A third of the oak *barriques* are renewed each year.

The presence of Jerome as wine maker and his philosophy on wine making suggests that the 'house style' at Château d'Aydie may be shifting a little to the fruitier end of the scale, even for the *Haut de Gamme*. It isn't the only change, a marketing consultant was hired to look at the business side of the operation and an issue that was highlighted was the company name. The suggestion was that customers needed to be able to identify wines from Château d'Aydie more easily and that consistency in labelling was needed. The result is the dropping of the name Laplace in favour of Château d'Aydie. This means that the Cuvée Frederick Laplace will now be renamed Ode d'Aydie, this must have been a difficult decision given the obvious pride the family have in their grandfather's memory and his place in the history of the *appellation*. At the time of writing I still have a supply under the original name.

The wines reflect the attention to detail in the wine making process from vine to glass. All the wines receive the same care and attention to produce excellent wines across the range.

The *Haut de Gamme* of the estate is **Château d'Aydie**, Madiran. It is made from 100% Tannat from vines aged over thirty years. The grapes come from Saint Lanne, Aydie and Moncaup, are hand-picked then fermented and macerated for five days at ten to twelve degrees, then macerated for a further twenty to twenty-five days. The ageing is in 225 litre oak *barriques* for between twelve and fifteen months and bottled after twenty months. The wine will age for ten years or more. It has had the reputation of being one of the more tannic and impenetrable wines in its youth, it does seem to be less so these days. Price ££

Ode d'Aydie, Madiran is also made from 100% Tannat from Saint Lanne and Moncaup. The grapes from the different parcels are vinified separately using the same process as the *Haut de Gamme*. This will drink a little earlier but will age well for five + years. Price £

Aydie l'Origine, Madiran is a blend of 70% Tannat and 30% Cabernet Franc. The grapes are from Saint Lanne and the varieties vinified separately. The grapes are macerated for between ten and fifteen days and the juice aged in steel tanks for eighteen months. This is a fruity style wine that will drink well in two to three years. Price £

Chapelle Lenclos, Madiran is 100% Tannat, macerated for up to thirty days. It is aged for between fifteen and twenty months in tanks and *barriques*. It will age for five years +. Price £

The **Mouréou**, Madiran is a blend of 60% Tannat, 20% Cabernet Franc and 20% Cabernet Sauvignon. The hand-picked grapes are macerated for five days, 75% of the juice is aged in tanks *sur lies* and 25% in oak *barriques* for twelve months. This is ready to drink earlier than the Chapelle Lenclos and will age for up to five years. Price £

The Pacherencs at the Château are of the same outstanding standard as the Madirans, Cuvée Frederic Laplace now marketed as Ode l'Aydie , one of the very best dry Pacherencs is made from 40% Arrufiac, 25% Gros Manseng and Petit Courbu with 10% Petit Manseng completing the blend. Price £.

The Pacherenc Moelleux, Château d'Aydie is made from Petit Manseng and as one would expect is up there with the best of the *moelleux* wines. Price £.

Maydie is a fortified wine based on a 'treat' devised by Frederic Laplace in the 1940s where *eau de vie* was added to grape juice

Tastings:

Château d'Aydie 2010, Madiran.
100% Tannat
Deep ruby. Blackcurrants and blackberries with some vanilla, slightly medicinal. On the palette there are dark black fruits, tar and a hint of prune. This is very young and needs time to integrate and develop. I expect this to become very good indeed.
January 2014

Odé d'Aydie 2009, Madiran.
100% Tannat.
Deep ruby. Aromas of ripe blackcurrants and liquorice on the nose. Reflected on the palette with added depth from the oak. Silky tannins, lovely mouth feel. Classic Madiran with more to come.
January 2014

Aydie L'Origine 2010, Madiran.
70% Tannat, 30% Cabernet Franc.
Medium ruby, cherries and a little raspberry on the nose. Good ripe red fruits and a little spice. This is a good example of modern Madiran, it went very well with duck at a canal side restaurant in the lovely town of Nerac.
June 2013

Domaine Mouréou 2010, Madiran.
60% Tannat, 20% Cabernet Franc, 20% Cabernet Sauvignon.

Medium ruby. Aromas of red fruits and hints of cherry. On the palette both Red and black fruits. Fruity and definitely for early drinking. Similar to Aydie L'Origine. Wine that definitely needs food to bring out its best.
September 2013

Chapelle Lenclos 2008, **Madiran.**
100% Tannat
Deep ruby. Prunes and blackcurrants on the nose, hints of spice, and meatiness on the palette to go with ripe fruit. Tannins are still a little intrusive and I would suggest that this needs a good two or three years to come together. Possibly an acquired taste, but good potential.
January 2014

Cuvée Frederic Laplace 2009, **Pacherenc Sec**.
40% Gros Manseng, 25% Petit Courbu, 25% Arrufiac and 10% Petit Manseng.
Pale straw yellow. Lovely grapefruit, pineapple and passion fruit aromas. Mineral palette with grapefruit and white peach. Elegant and restrained, well defined and well balanced fruit and acidity. Long. One of the best in the *appellation*.
February 2012

Terroir at Saint Lanne. Pebbles suspended in the clay.

CHAPTER 7

THE PHENOMENON THAT IS ALAIN BRUMONT

Alain Brumont
Château Bouscassé
32400 Maumusson-Laguian
Gers

Château Montus
65700 Castelnau-Rivière-Basse
Hautes-Pyrénées
Tel: +33 (0)5 62 69 74 67
Email: contact@brumont.fr
Website: www.brumont.fr
Open at Château Bouscassé:
Monday to Friday: 9am to 12pm and 2pm to 6pm.
Saturday: 9am to 12pm and 2pm to 6pm from mid-June to the end of August.
Closed Sundays.
437 hectares, Madiran, Pacherenc, Vins de Pays.
Production: 2 500 000 bottles.

Alain Brumont is arguably the driving force behind the renaissance of Madiran, but unlike some of the other winemaking families the transition from one generation to the next was not an easy one. Alain was enthused with the possibilities for Madiran following a visit to Bordeaux; his father however did not share his views. Alban Brumont was more farmer than *viticulteur*, only sixteen of one hundred and forty five hectares were under vine. Maize was a more reliable source of income than the risky business of making quality wines; his own wine production was based on high yields of Tannat blended with Merlot. Alain started to plot his future by taking on the derelict Château Montus, although there was a magnificent *chai* at the property the vineyard had been left in a very poor state. This may have been a blessing in disguise as it gave Brumont a clean canvas on which to develop his vision. However the process of raising money to buy the property may not have eased family relations; the local bank refused to approve credit for the project, Alain's father was on the board of the bank at the time!

Within five years he produced a wine that caught the eye of experts in Bordeaux who called it "the best Madiran ever." The press were quick to pick it up as "the wine of the decade" and a legend was born. The wine was the Château Montus **Prestige** 1985. However it was a fight to get the *cuvée* recognised as Madiran as, at the time, 100% Tannat wines were not within the A.O.C. regulations. It was the weight of the influence of the Bordelais that tipped the balance in his favour. Brumont had put his money where his mouth was, putting his faith in the Tannat grape and the use of new oak. The reviews were unprecedented for a Madiran, whether they were warranted is a moot point, Brumont was off and running. Never one to stand still he was anxious to expand and improve his holdings. He inherited seventeen hectares and the property at Château Bouscassé from his father in 1988 and he set about building a new underground *chai*, 1200 m2 in size. He repeated this at Château Montus in 1995, where the state of the art facilities are the envy of many illustrious estates throughout France. These projects came at a cost and his financial problems have been well documented, although that is now behind him and his vision for a hotel and conference centre at Château Montus has been shelved.

Brumont was determined to build a portfolio of the best *terroirs* on which to develop his winemaking. The Brumont family had land but much of it was good for growing maize but not for vines, he went about a prospecting exercise to find the best plots. The problem with this was it tended to be on other peoples land. In an interview with Andrew Jefford for Decanter magazine he revealed that he would go out at night making holes in fields with a mechanical digger; he was looking for clays, pebbles, iron and manganese. One can imagine that this would not have made him very popular, so much so that on occasion he had to use 'front companies' to close deals with people who refused to do business with him personally. He used field of maize in exchange or as part payment, these transactions would benefit both parties as arable land has the potential to generate higher profits than vineyards and Alain Brumont was only interested in wine.

This policy has worked well, Brumont owns four hundred and thirty hectares mostly on the best *terroirs*. Brumont and others acknowledge that many of the best *terroirs* are on the high ground, there are twenty two hills within the appellation boundaries and Brumont has land on twenty of them.

High density planting is the rule in the vineyard, when winemaker Fabrice Dubosc appeared on the scene he and Brumont set about doubling the density on some of the best sites This, along with green harvesting, enables the production of smaller bunches of grapes with more concentrated flavour. The rows of vines are orientated in such a way as to point to the sun at 3pm to give consistent exposure, no insecticides are used and where possible vineyards are separated by woodland to prevent contamination from treatments on other vines or crops. In addition ploughing is kept to a minimum to lessen the risk of upsetting the balance of bacteria in the soil. The land is treated using his own recipe of cow, sheep and horse manure mixed with crushed stones and pumice. Brumont is convinced that the lack of major industries and cities in the area is beneficial for the vines and he is keen to ensure that any water used is free from contaminants.

He is receptive to ideas from his staff and encourages them to air opinions and constructive criticism although I believe staff turnover is quite high. There are in the region of fifty staff split between the properties with another forty seasonal workers employed during the *vendange*, this is a major operation producing up to 2.5 million bottles a year.

Les Jardins de Bouscassé

The vineyards and production are split between two main properties, Château Montus at Castelnau-Rivière-Basse and Château Bouscassé, located at Maumusson-Laguian. The terroirs of Château Montus are on steep stony slopes, the best at La Tyre near Saint Lanne which occupies twelve hectares of land that faces south west. It is planted with 68 000 Tannat vines, complete with a ten metre, Hollywood style sign and a tree house that gives wonderful views over the Bergons valley. The vineyard is a comparatively recent addition and although originally just populated with Tannat vines a small amount of Cabernet Sauvignon has been added recently. The **La Tyre** *cuvée* is the flag bearer for what Brumont refers to as his 'left bank' property; he actually produces three all Tannat wines on *terroirs* in this area. Another 100% Tannat *cuvée* is produced at Château Bouscassé where the *terroirs* are different in nature, being more gently sloping clays and limestone. Brumont refers to Bouscassé as his 'right bank' property, this nod to Bordeaux gives you an insight into his thinking and his relationship with his colleagues in Madiran. The prices he can command are on another planet, however I have hardly heard a word said against him or even an inference of jealousy or ill feeling in all my discussions with locals. There is plenty of evidence that Brumont has been very much a part of the development of Madiran as part of a generation of innovators, one of the prime movers who encouraged local *vignerons* to put their faith in the Tannat grape. His commitment is to the region and its wine and that is respected, even if some of his methods may differ from those of his colleagues.

An example of the of the way in which Brumont is able to operate in a way his fellow winemakers in the region cannot is in marketing; the Laplace family at Chateau d'Aydie have had to look very closely at labelling and market placement. Brumont however seems relatively immune to such considerations, Torus becomes Cirus and the supermarkets lap it up: being the market leader certainly has its benefits. There is also the ability to experiment with new *cuvées* and different grape varieties; a recent example is his **Pinot Noir d'Alain Brumont**, where Pinot Noir blended with just a little Tannat. Outside the A.O.C. regulations the wine is marketed as a *vin de pays* but commands twice to three times the price of most top range Madirans. Pinot Noir is not alien to the South West and it is an interesting idea although the blend is not unique, Bodegas Marichal in Uruguay make a splendid Tannat/Pinot Noir blend which co-incidentally is one of my favourite Uruguayan wines.

Brumont has continued to put his faith in the Tannat grape and in the use of oak to compliment the variety in making great wine although he has tempered the use of new oak somewhat. He is convinced that ripe fruit from the best *terroir*, carefully sorted and treated gently, has the potential to produce wines that avoid the criticisms often made of over oaked wines. Grapes are hand-harvested but this can be a slow process when using the shallow crates, that Brumont insists upon, to ensure minimum damage to the grapes. Whenever possible the best bunches are left out in the sun for a couple of days to help reduce the astringency of the juice. Any delays in the logistical exercise of the *vendange* can lead to bunches to be left on the warm *galets* for a few hours or even overnight. He eschews micro-oxygenation but has developed his own *auto-pigeage* system for turning over the grape skins and uses long maceration periods, generally twenty five days for Tannat and thirty days for Cabernet Sauvignon. He does not filter his wines and maintains the highest standards of cleanliness in his facilities, enabling him to minimise the use of sulphur in the wine making process.

Brumont makes superb Pacherencs, for the dry version he extols the virtues of Petit Courbu, used for its freshness and aromas. All but one of his sweet Pacherencs are made under the Bouscassé banner, all being made from 100% Petit Manseng. Three of these are late harvested, referred to as *Vendanges Tardives* and are named after the month of the harvest in the Napoleonic calendar, Vendemaire, Brumaire and Frimaire.

Les Menhirs, a vin de pays vineyard at Maumusson.

Keeping track of Alain Brumonts activities would be a book in itself. Currently there are Torus (Cirus), Château Segondine, Laroche Brumont and various Côtes de Gascogne wines made under the Brumont umbrella. Curiously two of these Côtes de Gascogne wines are Tannat, Merlot blends, **Menhir** and **Merlot-Tannat**, a throwback to his father's era perhaps, although the wines will be made with greater attention to detail and considerably lower yields.

Alain Brumont's pre-eminence in the eyes of the media and many wine experts should not detract from the achievements of the region's other wine makers. Brumont can command prices twice or three times that of the other top wine makers and his financial position allows investments, experimentation and exploration of new markets that his neighbours can only dream about. He has recently gone into the *en primeur* market, another first in the *appellation,* though others such as Château d'Aydie are now following suit. In a sense he is almost an appellation of his own, but the publicity he has courted and received has benefited Madiran as a whole and as a figurehead, his wines are there to inspire others. Raising the bar on quality is a good thing; *vignerons* like Brumont, the Laplace family, the Capmartin family, Didier Barré, Jean-Marc Laffitte, Alain Bortolussi, Catherine Dupuy and others continue to do this to the benefit of all.

Château Montus

The top Madiran *cuvée* at Montus is **La Tyre**, a single vineyard at the highest point of the *appellation*, provides the Tannat which is the sole variety used. The site near Saint Lanne is steeply sloping with large pebbles underlain by red clay, south west facing. The harvest is limited to four or five bunches per vine to ensure good concentration of flavour. These grapes are macerated for three to six weeks and fermented in wooden vats. The juice is then aged in 100% new oak *barriques* for between fourteen and sixteen months. The wine should be laid down for ten years and it may improve for years more. Price £££££££

Next is another 100% Tannat wine, **XL** from steep pebbly slopes underlain with clay on a south facing slope. Made in much the same way as **La Tyre** it is aged in new oak 400 litre *barriques* for forty months. This is the technique that Guigal uses to make his La Mondote *cuvée* at Cote Rotie. Age for ten years +. Again this does not come cheap, Price ££££££

The last of the 100% *cuvées* is **Prestige**, the *terroir* here has pebbles on layered orange and brown clays. The steep slopes are southern facing and are amongst

the highest in Brumont's ownership. Given the same treatment as **La Tyre** it will age for ten years and last a lot longer. Price ££££

Montus is a blend of Tannat and the two Cabernets from a similar site to the Prestige. The maceration lasts three to six weeks. Fermentation is in wooden vats and aged in oak, 60% to 80% of which will be new, for twelve to fourteen months. This should be left for five years before drinking. Price ££.

Montus is the only white wine of the Château. It is a blend of Petit Courbu and Petit Manseng from vines grown on clay/limestone terraces. The grapes are pressed slowly and gently and the juice aged *sur lies*. Ageing is carried out

Keeping tabs on the vines.

for fourteen to sixteen months in 600 litre *barriques*. Drink within three years to get the best from the Petit Courbu. Price ££

The estate makes a Vin de Liqueur, **Vintage**, made from 100% Tannat. The grapes are dried in shallow crates, then fermented at twenty eight degrees and aged in oak *barriques* for eight to twelve months. Sometimes *mutage* is necessary to fix the alcohol content. Price ££

Château Bouscassé

The top Madiran is the **Vieille Vignes**. As you might expect it is made from 100% Tannat with vines aged from fifty to one hundred years. The vines grow on clay and limestone ridges and marbled clay *grepp* soils. The grapes are macerated for up to six weeks and fermented in new oak *barriques, sur lies* for fourteen to sixteen weeks. The wine will age for ten years, Price £££

The other two Bouscassé Madirans are blends. **Argile** is made from Tannat, the two Cabernets and Fer Servadou. Fermented is in wooden vats after three to six weeks maceration and then aged in Oak, 30% of the *barriques* are new. The wine is then aged for twelve to fourteen months *sur lies*. The standard **Bouscassé** is aged in *barriques* and will be approachable within five years. Both priced ££.

Bouscassé produces no less than five Pacherencs. The only *sec* is Jardins de Bouscassé, again Brumont shows his faith in Petit Courbu, and the variety contributes 80% to the blend with the balance made up of Petit Manseng. Gentle, slow pressing and fermentation at sixteen to eighteen degrees is followed by ten to twelve months ageing *sur lies*. This maintains the freshness and aromas of the Petit Courbu. No wood is used. Drink young. The name is an homage to the garden at Château Bouscassé. However, the gardens remain a little run down. Come an Alain, get them sorted! Price £

The Pacherenc sweet wines are all made from Petit Manseng grown on clay-limestone soils. Les Larmes Celeste, is vat fermented and aged *sur lies* in *barriques* for six months. This is a relatively simple sweet wine but it will last. Price £.

The other three *moelleux* style Pacherencs are handpicked and use *passerillage*, the grapes are left to desiccate to concentrate the sugars even further. Vendemaire is made from grapes picked in October, and aged for twelve months in *barriques*. As with the other *Vendange Tardives* wines the fermentation sometimes has to be interrupted to maintain the proper balance. This will age for five years, Price ££.

Brumaire uses grapes picked in November and will age for ten years and more. Maturity adds complexity to the aroma and flavour. Price £££. The third and finest of the *Vendange Tardives* Pacherencs is Frimaire. It is made from grapes picked in December and only produced when the conditions are perfect. This has occurred on five occasions up to press, 1994, 1995, 1996, 2000 and 2001. It is aged in new oak and should be left to its own devices for at least ten years. Price ££££.

Brumont also makes A.O.C. wines under three other *Domaines*. There are three wines under the **Torus** banner, a Madiran blend, a *vendage tardives doux* and a *sec* all priced £. There are two Madirans under the name Laroche Brumont, **Eglise** and **Grange**, Tannat, Cabernet Franc blends from different *terroirs*, Priced £. Finally there is Château Segondine, **Sacre Coeur**, a Madiran also made from Tannat and Cabernet Franc. Price £. Monsieur Brumont has particularly high hopes for Château Segondine, but this is definitely one for the future as the vines are still very young.

The **Pinot Noir d'Alain Brumont** is included here as I find the wine intriguing and it is seen as a very serious wine with a serious price tag. Pinot Noir is not totally alien to this region but this is the first commercial wine of its type produced here for many years. Price £££.

There are a number of Côtes de Gascogne wines, including a rosé. These exhibit the same attention to detail and meticulous wine making as the more esteemed A.O.C. wines.

Tastings:

Château Montus

La Tyre 2003, Madiran.
100% Tannat.
Dark garnet. Aromas of black and red fruits, hints of basil and oak.
On the palette smooth blackcurrant, mocha and liquorice with a slightly herbal background. This has lovely balance, elegant with silky tannins and deep, expressive fruit. Complex and fine. In some ways this is unrecognisable as Madiran whilst maintaining Tannat typicity.
August 2013

XL 1999, Madiran.
100% Tannat.
Very deep garnet, sweet blackcurrant, chocolate and pencil shavings on the nose. Flavours of prunes, liquorice and sour cherries. Good length and depth and complexity. Refined and maintaining good fruit.

December 2013

Prestige 1995, Madiran.
100% Tannat.
Deep and glossy ruby colour with aromas of pencil shavings, raspberry jam and spice. Red fruits with underlying black cherry. Almost Bordeaux like.
Well evolved, silky tannins, a rival to classed growth Bordeaux.
August 2012

In 2008 another bottle of the **Prestige 1995** was enjoyed alongside the following wines. Chante Allouette, Chapoutier, 2004, Pichon Longueville Comtesse de Lalande, 1997 and Château d'Yquem 1990. All three tasters agreed that the Montus, served after the Paulliac, held its own against these world class wines.

Prestige 1999, Madiran.
100% Tannat.
Deep garnet. On the nose, pencil shavings and sweet red fruits.
On the palette, spiced red and black fruits, long finish and rounded tannins
Another fine example of a top class Madiran.
January 2013

Château Montus 2007, Madiran.
80% Tannat, 20% Cabernet Franc/Sauvignon.
Dark purple colour, with aromas of red fruits, blackcurrant and cedar wood. On the palette flavours of blackcurrant, spice. Round tannins.
Excellent.
April 2013

Le Pinot Noir d'Alain Brumont 2009.
Pinot Noir with a little, (3%), Tannat.
Pale to medium brick in colour. Aromas of raspberries, mushrooms and *sous bois*. Lovely red fruits with a little sweetness and added spice. Darker fruit, almost prune like on the finish. This is elegant and Burgundian, perhaps comparable to a Volnay. Very, very good. Although I am not sure the Tannat is needed.
February 2014

Château Montus 2008, **Pacherenc Sec.**
Petit Courbu, Petit Manseng.
Straw yellow in colour with aromas of grapefruit and elderflowers.
On the palette flavours of lime, grapefruit and wet stones. Oily consistency with good fruit and underlying minerality. Exotic and elegant. Very good
September 2012

Château Bouscassé

Vieille Vignes 2004, Madiran.
100% Tannat.
Deep purple.   Sweet liquorice, sous bois and hedgerow. Good sweet
blackcurrant fruit, liquorice and leather. Quite sweet and soft, tannins still
present but quite rounded. This is a very refined in the context of Bouscassé
which is often seen as the more rustic *domaine*.
March 2013

Chateau Bouscassé 2006, Madiran.
50% Tannat, 26% Cabernet Sauvignon, 24% Cabernet Franc
Deep garnet, blackberries, cedar wood, leather and a hint of fennel.
On the palette flavours of raspberries and herbs. Soft and very 'right bank'.
Very good.
May 2012

Jardins de Bouscassé 2009, **Pacherenc Sec.**
80% Petit Courbu, 20% Petit Manseng.
Medium straw yellow. Gooseberries, sweet vanilla and soft spice on the nose.
On the palette it is floral with limes and hints of honey. Underlying gooseberry
and exotic fruits. Elegant Petit Courbu with Petit Manseng in the mid palette
and good acidity on the finish. Lovely.
January 2014

Frimaire 2000, **Pacherenc Moelleux.**
100% Petit Manseng
Deep amber. Aromas of truffle, lemons an oranges gently spiced nutmeg.
Flavours of dried fruits and truffles. Perhaps more sherry like than the 2001.
Very good length and freshness. The 2001 is probably a little better on its own,
this vintage excels with salty cheese.
February 2014

Frimaire 2001, **Pacherenc Moelleux.**
100% Petit Manseng
Deep amber. Aromas of marmalade, apricot confit, Christmas pudding, truffle.
On the palette confit oranges, apricots, lemon and truffles. This wine has great
depth and complexity, not at all cloying and is very long. This is an absolute joy
with Roquefort, desserts or for sipping on its own. A serious challenge to top
Sauternes.
March 2013

CHAPTER 8

CHÂTEAU LAFFITTE-TESTON, CAVES AND QUALITY

Château Laffitte-Teston
Jean-Marc Laffitte
32400 Maumusson-Laguian
Gers
Tel: +33 (0)5 62 69 74 58
Email: info@laffitte-teston.com
Website: www.laffitte-teston.com
Open: Monday to Friday 9am to 12.30pm and 1.30pm to 6.30pm.
Saturday: 10am to 12.30pm and 2pm to 6.30pm.
40 hectares, Madiran, Pacherenc , Vins de Pays.
Production: 250 000 bottles.

This is a beautiful estate, adjacent to Château Bouscassé, in what can arguably described as the heartland of Madiran wines, Maumusson-Laguian. The cement was barely dry on our first visit to the new tasting room which gives panoramic views over the vines. You can admire the vista and enjoy a lovely selection of wines in the cool airy space whilst the wines benefit from their temperature controlled

The tasting room at Laffitte-Teston

environment in the newly completed underground cellar. With the new there is the contrast of some very old Tannat vines, now nearing their 90th year. The elegant building may not rival the architecture of Château Viella but it is a marvellous setting looking down to the Route de Vignoble in the valley below.

The vines, with an average age of thirty years are sited on clay limestone soils. The vineyard holdings have risen to over forty hectares, thirty two hectares for Madiran and eight for Pacherenc. However in the past the land holdings were much higher, in the region of seventy hectares. Like Alain Brumont, Jean-Marc has sought out land with the best *terroirs* for the production of high quality wines and used his arable holdings as payment. The result may be the same but Jean-Marc's methods have not been controversial.

Jean-Marc's expertise in the vineyard and the *chai* produces wines of a consistently high standard. For the Pacherencs there is an unusually high proportion of Petit Manseng, though common in sweet wines it also dominates the blend in the dry *cuvée*. Jean-Marc Laffitte is self-taught but that has not proved to be any disadvantage, perhaps the opposite as his wines are very highly regarded and more accessible than most. Daughter Ericka and son Joris having completed oenological studies now assist Jean-Marc, they are the fifth generation of the family to work on the estate.

Innovation and a commitment to quality has become a feature of the *appellation* and Laffitte Teston is a good example. The investment in the tasting room and cellars is impressive but Jean-Marc has not rested on his laurels. In 2011 he began an experiment in the Grottes de Bétharram following a chance meeting with the curator Albert Ross which led to discussions about ageing Madiran in oak *barriques* in the caves.

The caves near the Gave de Pau close to Lourdes have been a tourist attraction since 1880's, some of the earliest visitors were British residents in Pau. In 1903 the caves were officially opened to the public and have remained very popular with an estimated 200 000 visitors a year. It is thought that the galleries will provide an ideal environment for ageing wines with a constant temperature of thirteen degrees and 100% humidity. Jean-Marc thought that this was an excellent opportunity to compare the ageing process of the wine in a natural environment, to that in his artificially controlled facility back in Maumusson. The wine will be tasted and compared to similar wines from the cellar by a panel of oenologists and the Laboratoire Départemental d'Eauze will carry out tests to highlight any discernible differences.

The process of delivering the wine to the caves was not without its challenges as stairs had to be negotiated, along with transportation by both train and boat through the various galleries, before reaching their destination beneath eight hundred metres of limestone. The first seven of twenty *barriques* were filled on-site in February 2011 and the first signs are encouraging. Nnlike the chalk caves used for storing Loire wines and Champagne, here the rock is dense karst limestone more akin to caves used in Lebanon. The humidity is offset by the size of the caves which keeps them well ventilated. The first tests revealed that none of the wine barrels needed topping up, usually a proportion of the wine, 'the angels' share' is lost to evaporation, not so here due to the high humidity and non-porous rock. The first wines are said to be lighter in colour and more elegant and supple than the wines back at the Laffitte Teston cellar, suggesting that the wine from the Grottes de Bétharram will be ready to bottle at an earlier stage. The *cuvée* is now available and the initial experiment deemed a success but whether this will become a long term project is still to be decided.

Jean-Marcs wines are some of the most widely available in the *appellation*, popular on wine lists in local restaurants they are also exported to over twenty countries worldwide. There are three Madirans produced; the *Haut de Gamme* **Vieille Vignes** is made from 100% Tannat and is aged in oak *barriques* for thirteen months. It has good ageing potential, from five to ten years. Price £.

The second *cuvée*, **Reflets du Terroir,** is made up of 80% Tannat, with 10% Cabernet Sauvignon and 10% Cabernet Franc. This is first aged in steel tanks and then in oak. This will be ready much earlier than the top *cuvée* but may improve for five years or more. Price £.

The final Madiran is named after Jean-Marc's son, perhaps to reflect the younger target market. **Cuvée Joris** is more of what I refer to as a 'wine bar' Madiran rather than a *Tradition*. It is made from 60% Tannat, 20% Cabernet Sauvignon and 20% Cabernet Franc. Part of the wine is aged in oak and some in stainless steel tanks. It is definitely an early drinking wine with the emphasis on fruit. Price £.

Named after Jean-Marc's daughter the Cuvée Ericka, Pacherenc Sec is made from 70% Petit Manseng, relatively unusual in a dry Pacherenc, the blend is then completed by the addition of 20% Gros Manseng and 10% Petit Courbu. It is aged in oak and can be drunk young or left for three or four years. Price £. The sweet cuvée is Reve d'Autumne, Pacherenc *Moelleux* made from 100% Petit Manseng. Again aged in oak *barriques* it is rated as one of the very best of its type. Price £.

There are two Vin de Liqueurs made here, the Tannat version of **Teston** is a rich port like liqueur made from overripe grapes that are fortified and aged for a year in barrel. The result is a smooth fruity *apéritif*, or if preferred, *digestif*. The **Teston** Blanc made from Petit Manseng is lighter and unique in the region.

Tastings:

Cuvée Grottes de Bétharram 2010, Madiran.
100% Tannat.
Medium/deep ruby, blackcurrant and vanilla on the nose. Blackcurrant and liquorice on the palette. The wood is still very evident and needs more time to integrate. Very good potential.
November 2013

Reflets de Terroir 2007, Madiran.
80% Tannat, 10% Cabernet Sauvignaon and 10% Cabernet Franc.
Deep garnet, black and red fruits on the nose. The palette is dominated by black fruits and a little oak. Nice depth and smooth tannins.
August 2013

Ericka 2010, **Pacherenc Sec.**
70% Petit Manseng, 20% Gros Manseng and 10% Petit Courbu.
Pale yellow with pineapple and exotic fruits on the nose. Passion fruit, melon and lemons. Good acidity. Lovely Pacherenc, elegant but full of flavour. Went well with food at the excellent Le Bartok, restaurant in Auch.
July 2013

Reve d'Automne 2008, **Pacherenc Moelleux.**
Deep amber, oranges and marmalade with a touch of spice on the nose. Seville oranges and quince on the palette. Lemons on the finish. Good acidity.
Classic, Pacherenc *Moelleux* with well integrated oak.
May 2013.

CHAPTER 9

DOMAINE PICHARD TRADITION IN ANGLO-FRENCH HANDS

Domaine Pichard
Jean Sentilles/Rod Cork
65700 Soublecause
Hautes-Pyrénées
Tel: +33 05 62 96 35 73
Email: pichard65@orange.fr
Website: www.domainepichard.com
Open: Monday to Saturday 9.30am to 12.30pm and 1.30pm to 6pm.
Sunday: by appointment.
12.5 hectares, Madiran and Pacherenc.

Domaine Pichard was created in 1955 by Auguste Vigneau. There are just over twelve hectares here, eleven split equally between Tannat and Cabernet Franc. The Pacherenc varieties are limited to Gros Manseng and Petit Manseng.

The Pyrénées and Adour valley from Château Pichard

The Madirans, particularly the top *cuvée*, are designed for the long term using long maceration periods and *élevage* in new oak *foudres*. There are older vintages still available that include a proportion of Cabernet Sauvignon from vines that were removed in 2007. The average age of the vines is around forty years.

The wines have been a favourite of The Wine Society subscribers for some years with both the **Tradition** and **Cuvée Speciale** being available. The *domaine* also exports to Japan and Korea.

Joint proprietor, Rod Cork is an Englishman, from St Annes in Lancashire. Although he now spends much of his time in Paris where he practises Law, he likes to leave the bustle of the city for the more relaxed environment of the vineyard. He has been visiting South West France since 1982 and his wife is from nearby Tarbes. When the property was made available in 2006 he, in conjunction with his brother-in-law Jean Sentilles, bought the property and set about making changes.

The new owners have a traditional view of Madiran and although they share the belief in Tannat as vital to the character and long term success of the wine they do not share in the enthusiasm for *cuvées* made from just Tannat. Similarly the current fashion for sweeter *moelleux* style wines does not find favour here; the traditional sweet wine with low levels of residual sugar similar to those found in Jurançon is preferred. There is no dry white wine made, again a traditional view shared by many in the Jurançon.

After purchasing the property the first three years were spent improving the vineyard. This included the removal of the Cabernet Sauvignon vines, the rational for this being that the *terroir* was unsuitable. This was supported by a geological survey by the University of Pau in the 1990's. The poor sandy clay soils are better suited to the growing Cabernet Franc as they are not dissimilar to some of the soils in the Loire valley vineyards. The low slopes also suit the growing of the Mansengs for lightly sweet Pacherenc.

Following the work in the vineyard there followed another two years of hard work to renovate the *chai*. The result is a very attractive *domaine* with the vines sweeping southwards, almost to the plain of the Adour valley, with stunning views of the Pyrénées. Wellington and his men would have trudged past this very spot on the 19th April 1814, no doubt pleased to see the valley opening up in front of them as they closed in on the retreating French army.

The **Cuvée Speciale,** although a 'premium' Madiran is made up of 70-90% Tannat and 10-30% Cabernet Franc giving it the potential for more red fruit flavours. The grapes are macerated in cement tanks for twenty to twenty eight days; *élevage* is in oak *foudres* and *barriques* for eighteen to thirty months. The average age of vines here is forty years. Older vintages may have some Cabernet Sauvignon in the blend, though these are becoming harder to come by. One would expect these wines to age for ten years or more but as with many other wines in the *appellation* the improvement in wine making techniques makes them approachable earlier than one might suppose.

The **Tradition** is just that, a traditional blend of between 55% and 60% Tannat, with the balance being made up of Cabernet Franc. The intention here is to produce a supple fruity Madiran but far from the early drinking 'wine bar' style.

The sole white wine Domaine Pichard is as described above, a Pacherenc *doux*. The blend of 70% Petit Manseng and 30% Gros Manseng unsurprisingly reflects the *encepagement* of the vineyard. The aim here is to balance a gentle sweetness with good acidity to produce a light elegant Pacherenc.

Tastings:

Cuvée René 2007, Madiran.
Deep ruby. Good depth of blackcurrant and liquorice fruit on the nose with plenty of red fruit. The palette reflects the nose with some tannins promising further development. Just entering the drinking 'window'. Very good.
January 2014

Tradition 1999, Madiran.
60% Tannat, 40% Cabernet Franc.
Medium to deep garnet with aromas of blackcurrant and pencil shavings.
On the palette more earthy, faded fruit and hints of liquorice. This is definitely a case of drinking a little too late. The fruit was fading in the glass but the bones of a good wine were still there.
August 2013

Domaine Pichard 2011, **Pacherenc Doux.**
Pale gold. Oranges with hints of green apple on the nose. Gently sweet oranges with good undertones of lemons and apples on the finish. A subtle wine that could be overpowered, so careful matching with food is required. Classic doux style, very enjoyable.
November 2013

CHAPTER 10

THE BERTOLUSSI FAMILY, ITALIAN ORIGINS, FRENCH TRADITION

Château de Viella
Alain Bertolussi
32400 Viella
Gers
Tel: +33 05 62 69 75 81
Email: contact@chateauviella.com
Website: www.chateauviella.com
Open: Monday to Saturday from 8am to 12.30pm and 2pm to 7pm.
Sunday: by appointment.
25 hectares, Madiran, Pacherenc and Vin de Pays.
Production: 180 000 bottles.

Just outside the village of Viella a splendid Château overlooks the valley, the vines sweeping down the slopes taking full advantage of this ideal location. This impressive estate is the property of the Bertolussi family who purchased it back in 1952 and is now amongst the most highly rated in the *appellation*.

Unlike many wine making families here the Bertolussi family are not from the region, they hail from the Frioul in Northern Italy. Pierre Bertolussi arrived in Viella in 1930 seeking work when there was none to be had in Italy. After a period working in the vineyard and sending money home to his family Pierre brought his wife Eleanore and young son Paul over to France. Times were hard in Viella also, with little money being made from wine the estate owners supplemented their income with arable farming. But for the Bertolussi family this was the opportunity they needed and when the owners decided to put the business up for sale Pierre was keen to buy it. Pierre's granddaughter, Claire explained that the idea of selling the estate to employees did not appeal to the owners and consequently to discourage the Bertolussis the price was increased. The situation was not resolved for ten years until the owners, unable to find another buyer finally agreed to sell and the Bertolussi family were able put down roots and plan for the future.

Alain Bertolussi took over from his parents in 1991 and immediately set about re-organising the vineyard. The best soils were identified and vines replanted. This was a slow process and the project was not completed until 2000 but this was the necessary groundwork for future improvements in the quality of the fruit and long term profitability of the *domaine*. The hard work and investment did not stop there, in 1995 a bottling and labelling machine was installed and the following year equipment was purchased to enable accurate temperature control of the must and wine. In 1998 micro-oxygenation equipment was installed; major investments with an eye to improving the quality and consistency of the winemaking. Alain is a very busy man, running the vineyard and the *chai as* he does not employ a wine maker.

Château Viella fully restored over-looking the vineyard

The *chai* has glass fibre tanks for the fermentation and maceration of the red wines, and cement coated tanks for the ageing of the **Tradition** and **Béarn** wines. There are 250 *barriques* for the ageing of the Madiran *cuvées* and for the fermentation of the Pacherencs.

In 2003 the renovation of the Château began. The project, which was completed in 2005, has added a new dimension to the estate. The 17th century building, formerly owned by the Marquis de Viella, was in a state of serious dilapidation and had previously been used as a holiday home by various absentee owners. The renovation was extensive with the top two stories being completely rebuilt and the existing structure being restored. Alain employed a company that specialises in traditional building methods to ensure a sympathetic restoration of what is an excellent example of the local architecture. The result is impressive, not only in its dominant position at the top of the hill but also in the way it has enabled the family to develop the business and contribute to the community of Viella.

On completion of the Château the next stage of the process was to create the *Jardins d'Aure* and the footpaths through the vines. The garden has a nice touch with plants representing the aromas and flavours of the wines produced at the estate. In summer events are held at the château; '*Viniscène*' is a series of evening musical events and '*Le Vin au fil des sens*' is a guided tour with a gourmet lunch, both of course involve the sampling of Château Viella's wines. The cool basement is used to store the *barriques* of Madiran wine; with the Château sited on the hillside the rear portion of the ground floor is essentially underground making the temperature easy to control.

Adjacent to the Château is the conciergerie and potage garden, this is the domain of Alain's mother, Henriette who loves to show people around. I am told that if no-one visits she has a tendency to phone down to the family and ask why. she is clearly very proud of the wine, the estate and the Château.

The estate retains the arable land that came with the original purchase, the scale of the operation is not a profit making enterprise but Alain is keen to hold onto the land for sentimental reasons.

Leaf removal in late June and early July

The hard work and sacrifice of previous generations means a lot here. 2013 proved to be a difficult year for maize and other arable crops across the region, spring started warm and then stalled. Many farmers in the south west had to replant, but then the weather turned hot, potentially damaging or killing the new plants whose roots had not had time to develop. This is a rarity, Alain could not recall another year like it.

The future of the estate seems assured, but who will be running the business when Alain retires is as yet, unclear. There are two daughters, Claire and Marion. It is clear that both are aware that there is pressure to take over, but not from their parents; it comes from a sense of obligation to the family. Claire returns home from University to help with the administration of the business and sales during the summer vacations; Marion runs the front office at the Maison des Vins in the village of Madiran. Both express a love for the home and the business; both have experienced the bright lights of the city but prefer the life here. There is a distinct sense of affection in the way they describe the wine growing community in the area, almost as if it were one family. I sense that the Bertolussi family will be here for some time yet.

Château Viella wines are of a very high standard. There are twenty five hectares under vine, twenty for red wines of which 65% is Tannat, the remainder split between Cabernet Franc and Cabernet Sauvignon, there is no Fer Servadou grown here. The five hectares of Pacherenc grapes are split 45% Petit Manseng, 35% Gros Manseng and 20% Arrufiac. The vineyard is essentially one plot but it encompasses different *terroirs*. The vines and *chai* being on one site is very convenient as Alain manages both.

Barriques of Madiran ageing in the cellar at Chateau Viella.

The *Haut de Gamme* at Château Viella is the **Prestige**. It is made from 100% Tannat from a four hectare plot of vines that have an average age of twenty five years. The soil is clay with limestone pebbles and the vines face south. The grapes are de-stemmed and macerated for twenty eight days, *élevage* is in new oak *barriques* for a period of twelve months in the cool cellar at the Château. The wine can age for ten years or more. It is as good value for money as any wine in the *appellation*. Alain recommends drinking this with game, lamb or venison and the *porc noir de Bigorre*. Price ££.

The next Madiran *cuvée* is the **Expression**, made up of 80% Tannat and 20% Cabernet Sauvignon. From a similar plot of four hectares this receives the same treatment as the **Prestige** and it will age for five years plus. Alain recommends grilled meats with this wine, couscous and even curry. Price £.

The **Tradition** is made from 60% Tannat, 30% Cabernet Franc and 10% Cabernet Sauvignon from a fifteen hectare plot with fifteen year old vines. The *terroir* here has clay soils with pebbles on the shallow south facing slopes. A third of the wine is aged in barrels the rest in tanks. This *cuvée* will be ready to drink earlier than the other *cuvées* due to the Cabernet Franc and the lighter soils. This wine is currently available on Brittany Ferries cross channel services. *Confit de Canard* and *Magret de Canard* are recommended for this wine. Price £.

There are three Pacherencs, a dry and two sweet, the Château Viella Pacherenc Sec is made from 60% Gros Manseng, 20% Petit Manseng and 20% Arrufiac. The wine is made from grapes on a one hectare plot of fifteen year old vines. The grapes are picked in October and *élevage* is in oak *barriques* for seven months. Price £

Château Viella, Pacherenc Moelleux is made from 100% Petit Manseng from a 1.5 hectare plot. The grapes are picked in mid-November and *élevage* is in oak *barriques* for seven months. It will age for up to ten years. Price £. The lighter sweet wine here is Louise d'Aure, Pacherenc Doux. 50% Gros and Petit Manseng are from a two hectare plot with vines aged an average of fifteen years. *Élevage* is in oak *barriques* for seven months. It is named after one of the previous owners of the Château who is remembered as being particularly kind to the poorer members of the community in Viella. It will reach its best within five years. Price £.

Vinosolis, is a Vin de Liqueur like those made at several other domains, uses very ripe Tannat.

Tastings:

Prestige 2010, Madiran.
100% Tannat.
Dark ruby, black fruits, hints of raspberry and vanilla on the nose. Blackcurrant and spice with a little red fruit and spice, good silky tannins developing. Quite long, some way to go to reach its best. Good potential.
November 2013

Expression 2005, Madiran.
80% Tannat, 20% Cabernet Sauvignon
Dark ruby, on the nose sweet black fruits, very ripe. On the palette robust black fruits, liquorice and spice. Pleasant, soft Madiran; excellent with red meat.
February 2013

Tradition 2010, Madiran.
60% Tannat, 30% Cabernet Franc and 10% Cabernet Sauvignon.
Deep ruby with prune sweetness, blackcurrant and spice on the nose. Black fruits and liquorice on the palette. Good example of the *Tradition* style.
Good and could have a little more to give in a year or so.
December 2013

Louise d'Aure 2012, Pacherenc Doux.
50% Gros Manseng, 50% Petit Manseng.
Pale to medium straw yellow in colour, aromas of *confit* oranges and lemon.
On the palette lightly sweet oranges with good lemon acidity. Very young.
July 2013

CHAPTER 11

THE CAPMARTIN FAMILY

Another influential family in the *appellation* are the Capmartins who have two estates in Maumusson-Laguian, both with excellent *terroirs* producing top class Madirans and Pacherencs.

Château Barréjat
Denis Capmartin
32400 Maumusson-Laguian
Gers
Tel: 05 62 69 74 92
Email:deniscapmartin@laposte.net
Website: www.chateaubarrejat.com
Open: Monday to Saturday: 9am to 12.30pm and 2pm to 7pm.
22 hectares, Madiran, Pacherenc and Vin de Pays.
Production: 150 000 bottles.

Barréjat is a twenty seven hectare estate adjacent to Château Laffitte-Teston and Château Bouscassé, arguably at the very heart of the *appellation*. It is run by Denis Capmartin whose father Maurice was the first to plant new Tannat vines in Maumusson. An exceptional feature of the estate is the plot of two hundred year old, un-grafted pre-phylloxera, vines used to produce the **Cuvée de Vieux Ceps**. Tannat dominates the blend with the balance of 20%, made up of the Cabernets. The *terroir* is sandy loam and gravel. It is aged in new oak.

Denis makes a 100% Tannat *cuvée,* **Cuvée de l'Extrême.** Again this is aged in new oak, the vines are fifty years old and again situated on loams. This needs longer ageing. **Séduction** is in the *Tradition* style with the Tannat dominating but with Cabernets making up 40% of the blend.

The Pacherenc Moelleux Cuvée de la Passion, is made from Petit Manseng and is aged for eighteen months in new oak. Price £.

Denis, whose brother Guy left the family estate to set up Domaine Capmartin took over the estate in 1992 and initiated changes, including the use of oak for ageing Madiran and Pacherencs. He has adopted the use of micro-oxygenation and *délestage* to soften the wines and had an underground *chai* built in which to age them. It is here that the differences of approach of the brothers are apparent, Domaine Barréjat wines lean towards a more modern style. I may be splitting hairs here as Denis' wines still require significant ageing but the results are a tad less masculine than his brothers.

Domaine Capmartin
Guy Capmartin
32400 Maumusson-Laguian
Gers
Tel. +33 (0)5 62 69 87 88
Email: capmartinguy@yahoo.fr
Website: www.domaine-capmartin.com
Open: Monday to Saturday: 9am to 1pm and 2pm to 7pm.
Sunday: by appointment.
18 hectares, Madiran, Pacherenc and Vin de Pays.
Production: 65 000 bottles.

Guy Capmartin bought 1.5 hectares of vines in 1987 to enable him to make his own wines after making wines with his family at Château Barréjat. Now he has eighteen hectares at his disposal, planted in high density and run on organic principles. The property is tucked away on the western slope of the ridge to the west of the River Bergons. There are 13.5 hectares for red and 2.5 for white AOC wines, with an average vine age of forty years. The soils are clay, gravel and *grepp* with some clayey limestone.

The fermentation room has cement tanks and Guy likes to balance the fruit and the effects of wood carefully to get the best out of the Tannat grape. The wines have a reputation of being traditional in nature with high levels of extraction; the top *cuvées* are powerful, dense wines which need time to reveal their masculine styled charms.

The *Haut de Gamme,* **Esprit de Couvent** is a 100% Tannat *cuvée* that is aged in 500L oak *barriques*. It will age for ten years or more. Price £££. Another premium Madiran is the **Cuvée de Couvent**. Again made from 100% Tannat, one should expect this to age for five to ten years. Price ££.

There are two Madiran blends produced, the first from the older vines is the **Vieille Vignes.** 70% of the blend is Tannat with 30% Cabernet Sauvignon. Age for five years or more. Price ££. The second is the **Tradition,** made with 50% Cabernet Sauvignon, 45% Tannat, and 5% Fer Servadou it is still an age worthy wine, as one would expect from the *domaine*. Price £.

The Domaine Capmartin, Pacherenc Sec is made from 80% Gros Manseng, 10% Petit Manseng and 10% Arrufiac. There are two sweet Pacherencs, both in the *moelleux* style; Domaine Capmartin is a blend of 80% Petit Manseng, and 20% Gros Manseng, the Cuvée de Couvent Doux is a premium 100% *Petit Manseng, Pacherenc Molleux* which deserves longer ageing.

Tastings:

Barréjat, **Cuvée de Vieux Ceps 2006**, **Madiran**.
80% Tannat, 20% Cabernet
Deep ruby, Sweet briar, blackcurrant and sweet liquorice on the nose. Blackcurrant, tar and spice on the palette. Oak well integrated with round tannins, good fruit and depth. Bought this in a *Hypermarché* for 5€50, shockingly cheap for such a good wine.
October 2013

Barréjat, Cuvée de la Passion 2009, **Pacherenc Moelleux**.
100% Petit Manseng.
Mid gold, *confit* fruits, vanilla and honey on the nose. Oranges and exotic fruits. Lemony acidity keeps it fresh on the palette, not at all cloying. Very good with salty blue cheeses. Great value for money
February 2013

Capmartin, **Cuvée du Couvent 2008**, **Madiran**.
100% Tannat.
Deep ruby. Dense blackcurrant and cedar on the nose, perhaps a little fennel. On the palette leather and blackcurrant, smoky. This is a brooding wine with years ahead of it and great potential. Imagine a log fire, a large hunk of meat and the howling of wolves, or am I getting carried away a little?
February 2014

Capmartin, Vielle Vignes 2008, **Madiran**.
70% Tannat, 30% Cabernet Sauvignon.
Deep garnet. Blackcurrant, wood shavings and prunes on the nose. Gentle spice and blackcurrant, tannins still a little obtrusive. Needs a little more time and it will improve.
April 2013

Capmartin, Tradition 2009, **Madiran**.
50% Cabernet Sauvignon, 45% Tannat and 5% Fer Servadou.
Deep ruby, black fruits and liquorice on the nose and reflected on the palette. A good solid *Tradition*. Still some drying tannins so it may need a little more time.
August 2013

CHAPTER 12

DOMAINE LAFFONT, CHINESE INVESTMENT, AMERICAN ENERGY

Domaine Laffont
Mr Chan/Stefano Yim
32400 Maumusson-Laguian,
Gers
4 hectares, Madiran and Pacherenc.
Production: 20 000 bottles.

Belgian Pierre Speyer may have had one of, if not the smallest estate in Madiran but his wines were very serious indeed. He had a total of just 3.9 hectares of vines clustered around his property; all but 0.6 hectares are for red wine. The average age of the vines is twenty five and are sited on clay soils with pebbles.

Pierre's wines were produced organically and meticulously using oak and natural yeasts. The wines are full bodied, masculine and benefit from long ageing and food. Despite the small size of the estate Pierre gained many plaudits for the consistency and quality of his wines. The use of the past tense is because Pierre sold the estate, a shame as Pierre is an interesting character.

But out with the old and in with the new, and that is Stefano Yim. Stefano is a sommelier hailing from the USA with origins in Hong Kong. He met Pierre three years ago and was impressed by his passion and his wines. They became friends and when Pierre decided it was time to move on Stefano was keen to move in. With financial backing from a Chinese businessman, a very long winded and bureaucratic process completed, he is now in a position to pursue his vision. His backer had been looking to invest in Bordeaux but Stefano convinced him to look further to the south.

Stefano established his wine business, The Nose, in Los Angeles in 2004. He believes that he was one of the first sommeliers to introduce Madiran to Los Angeles, a wine he had fallen in love with from his first taste. He loved the texture of the tannins and the uniqueness of the wine.

He wants to build on the foundations laid by Pierre, his mission is to get the very best from the Tannat grape. His focus is perfecting the pure Tannat *cuvées* but he does not underestimate the challenge and one senses he is very determined. He told me that he believes that "in a good year the complexity and longevity of a pure Tannat *cuvée* has the potential to outshine any top Bordeaux", a bold claim! Time will tell if he can achieve his goals. One of these is to end production of the **Tradition** *cuvée,* another is to develop the sustainable nature of the *domaine* and his intent is to use 100% native yeasts in the wine making process.

Stefano, the name was given to him by his Hispanic friends in Los Angeles, is not shy of standing out from the crowd or afraid of hard work. I look forward to tasting the fruits of his labours.

There were four Madiran cuvees produced by Pierre Speyer. **666,** made from 100% Tannat aged in Oak. Definitely for the long haul. Price ££££. **Hécate** another 100% *Tannat* wine was aged in new ok for 18 months. Keep for10 years + if you can find a bottle, price £££. **Erigone**, is a blend of 80% Tannat and 20% Cabernet Franc. The must was fermented in concrete vats before being aged in oak. Probably approachable much earlier than the two top *cuvees* if you are lucky enough to have one. Price ££. Pierre's **Tradition** was made from 50% Tannat, and 50% Cabernet Franc. Aged in old oak *barriques* it would be ready to drink early, for a Laffont. Price £

Domaine Laffont is a *moelleux* made from 100% Petit Manseng and aged in oak *barriques*. The production is small, in the region of four thousand bottles a year. Price ££.

Stefano Yim, the new proprietor of Domaine Laffont, at the 2013 vendange.

CHAPTER 13

INDEPENDENT PRODUCERS

Château d'Arricau Bordès
Paul and Alice Dabadie
64350 Arricau Bordès
Pyrénées-Atlantiques
Tel: +33 (0)5 59 68 57 14 or
+33 05 59 68 13 97
Email: alipaul@hotmail.fr
Open: weekend and week
days by appointment.

This small estate lies just up
the hill from the impressive
Château d'Arricau-Bordès, a
12th century. The vineyard is
an old one only recently
updated and planted with
Tannat, Cabernet Sauvignon,
Petit and Grand Manseng.
The Madiran as one would
expect given the blend is well
structured and a wine that
will be one to watch as the
vines age, the *terroirs*,

pebbly clays and limestone
also bode well for good
quality wines. Paul gave up

The Impressive Château d'Arricau Bordès.

farming to commit fully, not only to his own vines but also to the *appellation* as
a whole in his position as President of the Madiran growers association.

Tastings:

Château d'Arricau Bordès 2002, Madiran.
Dark garnet, prunes with a little strawberry on the nose. Blackcurrants and a
little prune and spice on the palette. A little faded but soft and enough fruit left
to enjoy.
July 2013

Château d'Arricau Bordès 2010, Pacherenc Moelleux.

Medium gold, candied fruit, oranges and apricots with gentle spice on the nose. *Confit* orange and soft oak with good acidity. Good fruit, acidity and length.
July 2013

Domaine de Barbazan
Thierry Casse
Impasse Barbazan 65700 Soublecause
Hautes-Pyrénées
Tel: +33 (0)5 62 96 35 77 or 06 14 31 35 91
Email: domainedebarbazan@yahoo.fr
Open: Monday to Friday 10am to 12pm and 2pm to 7pm, preferably by appointment.
Sunday: by appointment only.

The *Domaine* covers three hectares and has been certified organic since 2002. There are three wines each of these reflects the type of soil in each area of the vineyard. The vineyard was made up of Tannat vines in entirety, this presented a problem as the A.O.C. rules prevent wines being marketed as Madiran; the solution was for Thierry to rent some Cabernet Franc vines.

The *Haute de Gamme* of Domaine Barbazan is the **Vieilles Vignes** *cuvée*, these vines were planted in the 19th century, one of the very few pre-phylloxera vineyards still in existence. Made from 100% Tannat the wine has good ageing capacity probably up to ten years. Price £. The two other Madiran *cuvées* are produced on yellow clay and gravel with large pebbles. These will both drink much earlier than the **Vielles Vignes**.

Domaine de Bassail
Patrick Berdoulet
32400 Viella
Gers
Tel: +33 (0)5 62 69 76 62
Email: domainebassail@wanadoo.fr
Open: Every day 9am to 12.30pm and 2pm to 7pm.

The *Domaine* covers eleven Hectares, 10.25 of this is for Madiran with the balance for the production of Pacherenc. The Madiran vineyards face south and those for Pacherenc face south east. **Cuvée Saint-Vincent** is the top Madiran of the *Domaine*. It is made from 100% Tannat and will be approachable after five years. Price £, the other *cuvée* is the **Tradition**. The Pacherenc, Cuvée Muriel, is in the *moelleux* style made from 100% Petit Manseng, the grapes are picked in November which allows them to achieve maximum sweetness. Price £

Clos Basté
Chantelle and Phillipe Mur
64350 Moncaup
Pyrénées-Atlantiques
Tel: +33 (0)5 59 68 27 37
Email: closbaste@wanadoo.fr
Open: Monday to Friday 10am to 6pm. Saturday 10am to 6pm.
Sunday: by appointment.

Clos Basté consists of ten hectares, certified organic. There are 9.5 hectares of red grapes and just half a hectare of white, the average age of the vines is thirty years. The ethos here is to let the *terroir* shine through by hand picking the grapes, low yields and intervening as little as possible in the wine making process. The vineyard sits on clay limestone soils with large pebbles. The wines are gaining a reputation for their roundness and are considered soft by Madiran standards. Phillipe previously worked at Chateau d'Aydie.

Clos Basté is Phillipe and Chantelle's top Madiran. It is a 100% Tannat *cuvée* which is oak aged for twenty months and lightly filtered. It will age for five years and more. Price ££. **L'ésprit de Basté** is in the *Tradition* mould. Made from. 70% Tannat and 30% Cabernet Franc it is also aged in oak. The addition of the Cabernet Franc adds freshness to the fruit. Price £

Tasting:

Clos Basté 2010, Madiran.
100% Tannat
Deep ruby. On the nose this is almost Kirsch like, more cherry than black fruit certainly. On the palette red and black fruits but still a way to go to reach its best. Not sure how to rate this, it seems very different to many Madirans. Enjoyable and the potential to develop further.
February 2014

Domaine Bernet
Yves Doussau
32400 Viella
Gers
Tel: +33 (0)5 62 69 71 99
Email: earl.bernet@wanadoo.fr
Open: Monday to Friday 8am to 7pm. Saturday 9am to 7pm.
Sunday 9am-12pm

The *Domaine* consists of eleven hectares, nine hectares for Madiran and two hectares for Pacherenc. The vines are sited on some of the lighter soils of the appellation. Grapes are handpicked and the wines are aged in tanks. The **Vieille Vignes** *cuvée* is made with 80% Tannat, **Domaine Bernet** is 60 % Tannat. The *terroir* here probably doesn't lend itself to a premium 100% Tannat *cuvée*. The reputation here is for fruity Madiran.

Follow the signs and be assured of a warm welcome.

Domaine Bernet, Pacherenc Sec is made from 80% *Gros Manseng* blended with 20% Petit Courbu to add freshness. The sweet Pacherenc, Domaine Bernet tends towards the *moelleux* style with 80% Petit Manseng blended with 20% Gros Manseng, aged in oak barrels it has ageing capacity but can be enjoyed young.

Domaine Betbeder
Marie Hélène Dufreche and Jean Jegun
64330 Conchez de Béarn
Pyrénées-Atlantiques
Tel: +33 (0)5 59 04 00 54
Website: www.domainebetbeder.com
Email: domainebetbeder@orange.fr
Open: Monday to Saturday: 9.30am to 12pm and 2pm-6pm.

Sunday: by appointment

The *Domaine* has six hectares on south and south east facing slopes. It is run by father and daughter. There are five wines produced here four of which are A.O.C. wines. The **Vielle Vignes** is made with hand-picked grapes from sixty year old vines and will improve with 10 years ageing or more. It is made with 90% Tannat and 10% Cabernet Franc. Price £. The **Tradition** is made with 55% Tannat, 45% Cabernet Franc. The high proportion of Cabernet Franc gives the wine a lighter touch and can be drunk relatively young but it will age for five years. Price £.

The dry Pacherenc, Domaine Betbeder is made with an unusually high proportion of Arrufiac, up to 90% with the balance made up of Gros Manseng. Drink young. Price £. The sweet Pacherenc, Domaine Betbeder is another Pacherenc made in the *moelleux* style with a blend of 90% Petit Manseng and 10% Petit Courbu for freshness. It will age for up to five years. Price £.

Domaine des Bories
Vincent Chabert
64350 Crouseilles
Pyrénées-Atlantiques
Tel: +33 (0)5 59 68 16 24 or (0)6 79 65 43 49
Email: dom.desbories-madiran@orange.fr
Open: Every day from 10am to 5pm by appointment

Vincent Chaubert bought the *Domaine* in 2006 after having worked in Quebec for ten years and a further four years working for Alain Brumont at Château Montus. He has eleven hectares of vines from which he makes two Madirans and two Pacherencs. Vincent has managed to use his contacts to export wines to Canada and has his sights set on China.

The top Madiran is the **Vieille Vignes,** a blend of 80% Tannat, 20% Cabernet Sauvignon and Cabernet Franc. It will age for five to ten years. Price ££. The **Tradition**, made from 60% Tannat and 40% Cabernet Sauvignon and Cabernet Franc will mature earlier, price £.

Vincent produces a dry Pacherenc, Domaine des Bories and a sweet Pacherenc in the *moelleux* style again named simply Domaine des Bories. The *moelleux* Is made from Petit Manseng and will age but can be enjoyed young. Both Pacherencs are priced £.

Domaine Brana
Pierre Delle Vedove
32400 Maumusson-Laguian
Gers
Tel: +33 (0)5 62 69 77 70
Email: delle.vedove@hotmail.fr
Website: www.domainebrana.com
Open: Monday to Saturday: 9am to 12pm and 2pm to 7pm.
Sunday: by appointment.

The *Domaine* has seven hectares of vines situated adjacent to some of the top *domaines* in the *appellation* and though small in size there is a wide range of cuvees. There are no less than six Madirans and three Pacherencs.

The top three Madirans are **Cuvée Ta, Cuvée Elodie** and **Cuvée Essencia** all priced ££. **Fut des Chenes, Vieille Vignes** and **Sacre Coeur** are all priced £. There are two dry Pacherencs Cuvée Anais, price £ and Le Petit Secret de Brana, Price ££. The third Pacherenc is a Pacherenc Doux, price £

Domaine Coustau
Edmond Prechacq
64330 Mont Disse
Pyrénées-Atlantiques
Tel: +33 (0)5 59 04 02 46

The *Haute de Gamme* is **Cuvée Royale**, Madiran. It is aged in oak and can be cellared for up to ten years to show it at its best. Price £. The **Tradition**, made from70% Tannat, 30% Cabernet Sauvignon is a much fruitier wine. Price £. The Pacherenc Doux is gaining a good reputation for elegance.

Tasting:

Cuvée Royale 2009, Madiran.
Deep ruby, red fruits and vanilla on the nose with blackcurrants and liquorice dominating the palette. A litter bitter edge to the finish, definitely needs food. October 2103

Domaine du Crampilh
Bruno Oulié
64350 Aurions Idernes
Pyrénées-Atlantiques
Tel: +33 (0)5 59 04 00 63
Email: madirancrampihl@orange.fr
Open: Monday to Friday: 8am to 7pm. Saturday: 9am to 6pm.
Sunday: by appointment

The thirty hectares of vines are managed by Bruno Oulié who is the fourth generation of the family to do so. There are twenty hectares of Madiran and six of Pacherenc on south and south east facing slopes. The vineyard has grown significantly since the 1960's when the Oulié family were one of the last Madiran surviving growers as the *appellation* reached its nadir. The average age of the vines is thirty five years, sited on gravel clay and clay limestone soils.

Bruno varies the use of oak in his wines, the *Haut de Gamme*, **Vieille Vignes** uses new and used oak barrels; it is an age worthy wine made from 100% Tannat, price ££. There is no oak used in the *Tradition* style , **L'Original**; the blend is 70% Tannat and 30% Cabernet Sauvignon. Price £.

The sweetest of the wines, Celeste is a *moelleux* style Pacherenc, made from late harvested Petit Manseng and aged in oak barrels. The Tradition is a Pacherenc in the lighter *doux* style. It is a blend of 65% Gros Manseng, 18% Petit Courbu and 17% Arrufiac. The Domaine Du Crampilh, Pacherenc Sec. is a blend 25% each of Arrufiac, Petit Manseng, Gros Manseng and Petit Courbu.

Tastings:

Vielle Vignes 2006, Madiran.
100% Tannat.

71

Dark purple, the nose is all blackcurrant and liquorice, the blackcurrant is tempered with some red fruit sweetness on the palette. Silky tannins and well integrated oak and fruit. Very good.
August 2013

Tradition 2011, **Pacherenc Doux**.
65% Gros Manseng, 18% Petit Courbu and 17% Arrufiac.
Pale yellow, exotic fruits and a little honey on the nose. Peach with gentle sweetness. Simple sweet wine that's good with cheeses.
July 2013

Domaine Damiens
Pierre-Michel Beheity
64330 Aydie
Pyrénées-Atlantiques
Tel: +33 (0)5 59 04 03 13
Email: domainedamiens@numeo.fr
Website: domainedamiens.e-monsite.com
Open: Monday to Friday: 9am to 12.30pm and 2pm to 7pm.
Saturday and Sunday: by appointment.

In 1970 Andre Beheity bought ten hectares of land adjacent to the existing six hectares of vineyard, by 1980 the *Domaine* had twelve hectares under vine and this has now increased to sixteen hectares some of which are on steeper slopes and planted to a higher density than the older vineyards to enable smaller yields and better quality. The first bottling was done in 1971 and there has since been investment in modern equipment and a move to oak ageing.

This family run vineyard is gaining a growing reputation for its wines. It was certified organic in 2011, though no chemicals have been used in the vineyard for over fifteen years. The *Domaine* uses the *Methode Herody* of soil analysis and testing to achieve the right soil conditions for healthy and strong vines.
The *Haut de Gamme*, **Cuvée Saint Jean** uses grapes from old vines on the gravelly clay slopes, it is a 100% Tannat *cuvée*, aged for twenty four months and will start to show its best after five years, price ££. The **Tradition** uses grapes from silty alluvial soils, the blend adds 30% of blended Cabernet Franc and Cabernet Sauvignon to the Tannat to produce an earlier maturing wine. Price £.

The Domaine Damiens, Pacherenc Sec is a blend of 80% Gros Manseng and 20% Petit Manseng. Price £. The sweet Domaine Damiens Pacherenc is a *moelleux*; although it has a high percentage of Gros Manseng, 40%. The grapes are late harvested, sometimes into December which gives maximum sweetness. Aged in oak *barriques* it is worth setting aside in a cool place for a while. Price ££.

A *vins de liqueur* **Le Taheity,** is also produced, from ripe Tannat grapes. Price £.

Tastings:

Cuvée Saint Jean 2007, Madiran.
100% Tannat.
Deep garnet, on the nose aromas of cherries. Black and red fruits dominate with liquorice sweetness. This is good solid Madiran.
July 2013

Tradition 2010, Madiran.
70% Tannat, 30% Cabernet Franc and Cabernet Sauvignon.
Deep ruby with red fruits and blackcurrant on the nose. Hints of toffee. The palate is a pleasant mix of black and red fruits and sweet liquorice. Very good *Tradition* style, handled Chorizo with aplomb.
February 2014

Domaine Damiens 2011, **Pacherenc Sec**.
80% Gros Manseng and 20% Petit Manseng.
Pale yellow, grapefruit and lemons on the nose. Flavours of grapefruit and gooseberries with lemon acidity on the finish. Refreshing.
December 2013

Domaine Dou Bernes
Jean Paul Cazenave
64330 Aydie
Pyrénées-Atlantiques
Tel: +33 (0)5 59 04 04 49
Email: domaine.doubernes@orange.fr
Website: www.domainedoubernes.com
Open: Monday to Saturday: 9.30am to 7pm.
Sunday: by appointment

Dou Bernes is another *domaine* that has been owned by the same family for generations, Jean Paul has been running the business for over fifteen years. The fourteen hectares of Dou Bernes are split between ten of Madiran varieties, three of Pacherenc and one hectare for *vin de pays* rose wine. Jean Paul's wines aim to maximise the fruit from vines that grow in predominantly gravel clay soils.

There are three Madirans, a Tradition and two aged oak barrel aged *cuvées*. There are also three Pacherencs, one dry and two sweet. In addition a serious age-worthy Bearn rose is made from Tannat and Cabernet Franc.

Terroir de Rendoau, is the top Madiran made from 95% Tannat and 5% Cabernet Sauvignon. Aged in oak *barriques,* it is by reputation, a traditional slow maturing wine that will age ten to fifteen years. Price ££. **Dou Bernes** is 90% Tannat and 10% Cabernet Sauvignon, again aged in oak it will take five to ten years for the tannins to mature and the oak to integrate. Price £. The **Tradition** is made up of 70% Tannat, 20% Cabernet Franc and 10% Cabernet Sauvignon, it will mature far more quickly than the other *cuvées*. Price £

Domaine Dou Bernes, Pacherenc Sec is made from 40% Gros Manseng, 40% Petit Courbu, and 20% Arrufiac. It is fresh and will drink young. Price £.

The two other Pacherencs are in the *moelleux* style, Domaine Dou Bernes is made from 80% Petit Manseng and 20% Gros Manseng will improve with age but can be enjoyed young. Au Fil du Temps is 100% Petit Manseng and is best left to mature for up to five years. Both *moelleux cuvées* are priced £.

Tasting:

Terroir de Rendoau 2009, Madiran.
95% Tannat and 5% Cabernet Sauvignon.
Deep ruby, blackcurrant and a little vanilla oak on the nose. Blackcurrants and a little spice with a layer of soft vanilla. Well integrated elements, good.
November 2013

Clos de l'église
Arnaud Vigneau
64350 Crouseilles
Pyrénées-Atlantiques
Tel: +33 (0)5 59 68 13 46
Email: closdeleglise@orange.fr
Website: www.closdeleglise.com
Open: Monday to Saturday 8am to 12pm and 2pm to 7pm.
Sunday: by appointment.

There are twenty hectares of vines surrounding the family home in Crouseilles managed by Arnaud Vigneau. Arnaud is the fifth generation to produce wines at Clos de l'église, there are three Madirans and three Pacherencs to choose from.

Pur Sang is 100% Tannat and is aged in 100% new oak. This needs time for the oak to mellow, so set aside for five years +. Price ££. **Fut de Chêne,** as it suggests is aged in oak *barriques*. Due to it being a blend of 80% Tannat and 20% Cabernet Sauvignon and being aged in older *barriques* this will be ready to drink earlier than the **Pur Sang**. Price £. The **Tradition** is a blend of 60% Tannat, 30% Cabernet Franc and 10% Cabernet Sauvignon. It is aged in steel vats and is for relatively early drinking, price £

Clos de l'église**,** Pacherenc Sec made from 80% Gros Manseng and 20% Petit Manseng is for early drinking. Price £. Cuvée Marie is a *moelleux* made from 100% Petit Manseng and aged in oak *barriques*. It will age up to ten years but will be approachable far earlier. Price ££. The second sweet Pacherenc, Clos l'église leans further to the *doux* end of the scale, made up of 75% Petit Manseng and 25% Gros Manseng it does have the capacity to age but is lighter than Cuvée Marie. Price £.

Clos Fardet
Pascal Savoret
65700 Madiran
Hautes-Pyrénées
Tel: +33 05 62 31 91 37

Email: closfardet@gmail.com
Website: www.madiran-closfardet.net
Open: Monday to Friday from9.30am to7pm. Saturday from 9.30am to 6pm.
Sunday: by appointment

Pascal Savoret has developed Clos Fardet from the vineyard established by his grandfather Eugene Fardet. Pascal studied oenology at the Lycée Agri-Viticole de Blanquefort in Bordeaux and gained experience at Château Dillon, a *Cru Bourgeois* estate in Haute Medoc. On graduation he worked with Didier Barré at Domaine Berthoumieu.

The estate is a definite mix of old and new, the cellar dates back to the 1920's and includes an old *'cuvan presse'* which is still in use. Pascal believes the old equipment provides a gentler and more effective solution than some of the modern alternatives. However, Pascal does not eschew the modern; there are fibreglass tanks for fermentation and racking and a steel tank for the production of rosé wines and future production of Pacherenc. A great believer in the affinity Tannat has with oak, Pascal has added larger 400L *foudres* to existing oak *barriques*.

In the vineyard Pascal has been steadily adding to the original three hectares. He has added parcels of Tannat and Cabernet Franc and the most recent addition, planted in 2012, is a plot for the production of Pacherenc. In addition to two Madiran *cuvées*, Pascal also makes rosé with Tannat and **La Cuvée Beller,** made from *Cabernet Franc.*

Clos Fardet is a 100% Tannat *cuvée,* aged for 12 months in oak *barriques*. Look to age this for up to 10 years. Price ££. **La Barrique Oubliée** is a premium Madiran made from 100% Tannat. It is aged for 6 years in *foudres* and sold in magnums. Price ££££

Tasting

Clos Fardet 2010, Madiran.
Tannat, Cabernet Franc.

Mid ruby. Black and red fruits on the nose. Gently spiced palette, elegant.
February 2014

Château De Fitere
Rene Castets
32400 Cannet
Gers
Tel: +33 (0)5 62 69 82 36
Email: vignoble.fitere@aliceadsl.fr

Rene Castets took over the estate at the tender age of nineteen due to his
father's illness but he has taken to the task with great energy. He has enlarged
the estate to a total of twenty three hectares and produces a wide range of
cuvées including Côtes de Gascogne wines.

There are four Madiran cuvees, **Vieille Vignes, Cuvée Cour Cannet, Cuvée
Manade** and a **Tradition.** The **Tradition** is made from 70% Tannat and 30%
Cabernet Sauvignon. It is aged in steel vats, it will be approachable on release.
Price £. Cuvée Karine, is a Pacherenc Doux made from a blend of Petit
Manseng, and Gros Manseng.

Château Floris
Gabriel Hugues
64350 Moncaup
Pyrénées-Atlantiques
Tel: +33 (0)5 59 68 17 64
Email: sales@chateaufloris.com
Website: www.chateaufloris.com

This estate has ten hectares under vine, the handpicked grapes are de-
stemmed and fermented in steel tanks to maximise the fruit. **Château Floris** is
made from 67% Tannat, Cabernet Sauvignon, Cabernet Franc and a little Fer
Servadou. It should be ready to drink after five years. Price £.

Domaine de Grabiéou
Frédéric Dessans
32400 Maumusson

Gers
Tel: +33 (0)5 62 69 74 62
Email: contact@domaine-de-grabieou.fr
Website: www.domaine-de-grabieou.fr
Open: Monday to Saturday 9am to 7pm.
Sunday: by appointment.

This twenty hectare estate was completely replanted in the 1960s and 1970s. There are three Madirans; **Prestige** is made from 100% Tannat. Price ££. **Tradition** is a blend of 60% Tannat and 40% Cabernet. Price £. There is also an easy drinking Madiran, **La Cavette.** Price £.

Domaine de Grabiéou, Pacherenc Sec is made from a blend of Gros Manseng and Petit Courbu and is very fresh in style. Price £. Domaine de Grabiéou is a *moelleux* made from 100% Petit Manseng. The grapes are hand-picked in December and aged in oak *barriques*. Price £

Domaine d'Héchac
Jean Pascal and Fabien Remon
65700 Soublecause
Hautes-Pyrénées
Tel: +33 (0)5 62 96 35 75 or (0)6 82 16 99 78
Email: domainehechac@wanadoo.fr
Open: Monday to Saturday 9am to 7pm.
Sunday: by appointment only

The estate consists of seventeen hectares, situated just across the road from Domaine Pichard. The Madirans are **Cuvée Le Marquis,** named after the previous owner the Marquis de Tranclieu, it is aged in oak and will cellar for five to ten years. Price ££, **Cuvée les Aspalières,** again oak aged is in the *Tradition* style. Price £. There are two Pacherencs, Cuvée Maelys, Pacherenc Sec, price £ and Cuvée Maelys, Pacherenc Doux, price ££.

Tastings:

Cuvée Le Marquis 2008, Madiran.

Deep ruby, aromas of blackcurrants and oak. Blackberries and blackcurrants with underlying red fruit. Very solid Madiran, smooth tannins. Needs food.
July 2013

Cuvée les Aspalières 2010, Madiran.
Tannat, Cabernet Sauvignon and Cabernet Franc blend.
Deep ruby, sweet cherry nose. Blackcurrant and red fruits on the palette. Easy drinking.
July 2013.

Domaine Hourcadet
Nathalie and Christian Hourcadet
64350 Aurions-Idernes
Pyrénées-Atlantiques
Tel: +33 (0)5 59 04 01 98 or (0)6 33 80 51 36
Email: hourcadenathalie@wibox.fr
Open: Monday to Saturday 8.30am to 7.30pm.
Sunday: 10am to 6pm.

Domaine Hourcadet has just less than eight hectares, six of these are dedicated to Madiran and the remainder to Pacherenc. The red grape varieties, Tannat and Cabernet Sauvignon grow on clay and limestone soils. The whites, Gros and Petit Manseng, Petit Courbu and Arrufiac grow on stony soils giving them lightness and elegance.

Domaine Labranche Laffont
Christine Dupuy
32400 Maumusson-Laguian
Gers
Tel: +33 (0)5 62 69 74 90
Email: christine.dupuy@labranchelaffont.fr
Website: www.abistodenas.com
Open: Monday to Friday from 9.30am to 12.30pm and 2pm to 6.30pm by appointment.
Saturday and Sunday: by appointment only

Christne Dupuy has managed this twenty hectare estate since 1993 after studying oenology in Toulouse. Since that time the estate has doubled in size with seventeen hectares of Madiran, Tannat having 70% with the remainder split equally between the Cabernets. The three hectares of Pacherenc vineyard is split equally between Gros and Petit Manseng. Most of the vines are in Maumusson, some of which are pre-phylloxera vines which help create the estates *Haute de Gamme*. Other vines are situated at Saint Lanne on the other side of the valley. The vines here are, on average, aged between thirty five and forty years and sited on silty clay and clay limestone soils.

Christine is committed to low yields and producing wines that reflect the character of the soils. Recently she has been experimenting with biodynamic methods in part of the estate. The wines have a reputation for being refined and more feminine than most within the *appellation*.

The **Vieille Vignes** is a serious age-worthy Madiran. It is made from 100% Tannat including some pre-phylloxera vines. It is aged in oak *barriques* for twenty four months. It will undoubtedly age for up to 10 years, however given the reputation for the elegance of the Madiran produced here I would expect this to be very drinkable earlier than this. Price ££. The **Tradition** is made from a blend of 60% Tannat and 40% Cabernet Franc. Age 5 years. Price £

The Labranche Laffont Pacherenc Sec, is made from 70% Gros Manseng, 20% Petit Manseng and 10% Arrufiac. It is aged in oak for five to eight months. As with most of the dry Pacherencs this will drink young, however it will keep, allowing the oak to integrate and add to the complexity. Price £. The other Pacherenc is labelled Pacherenc Doux however as it is made from 100% Petit Manseng it definitely has its feet in the *moelleux* camp. Accordingly it will have the potential to age for up to ten years. Price ££.

Tastings:

Vieille Vignes 2010, Madiran.
100% Tannat
Deep garnet. On the nose layers of red and black fruits. The palette shows good fruits and underlying hints of leather. This needs time but has excellent potential.
September 2013

Domaine Labranche Laffont 2012, **Pacherenc Sec.**
70% Gros Manseng, 20% Petit Manseng and 10% Arrufiac.
Medium gold, grapefruit dominates the nose. Gooseberries, grapefruit and a little oak on the palette. Good but will improve with a little more age.
July 2013

Domaine Labranche Laffont 2011, **Pacherenc Doux.**

Petit Manseng.
Medium gold. Oranges and marshmallow on the nose. Confit orange intensifying through the mid-palette, citrus acidity on the finish. Although marked as Doux this is in the *moelleux* style. Very intense oranges but should develop further. Good with potential to be very good.
January 2014

Domaine Laougué
Pierre Dabadie
32400 Viella
Gers
Tel: +33 (0)5 62 69 90 05
Email: pierre-dabadie@orange.fr
Website: www.domaine-laougue.fr
Open: Monday to Saturday 9am to 7pm.
Sunday 9am to 12pm.

Pierre has sixteen hectares of vines. He possesses some very old Tannat vines from which he produces the top *cuvées*. He uses oak throughout the range but by reputation and my own observation the wood is very well handled giving well rounded and early maturing wines. I have been very impressed with Pierre's wines, they are beautifully made and up there with the best.

There are four reds, **Passion de Charles Clément** made from 100% Tannat is aged in new oak *barriques*. It will age for ten years. Price £££. Next is **L'Excellence de Marty** a blend of 80% Tannat, 10% Cabernet Sauvignon and 10% Cabernet Franc. Half is aged in tank and the other half in new oak. You should expect this to be ready in five years. Price ££. **Le Clos Camy** made from 50% Tannat, 35% Cabernet Franc and 15% Cabernet Sauvignon is aged in tank, price £. The other *Tradition* style Madiran made here is **Domaine Laougué** a blend of 50% Tannat, 25% Cabernet Franc and 25% Cabernet Sauvignon. Price £.

Passion de Charles Clément, Pacherenc Sec is made from 100% Petit Courbu. And aged in oak, quite a difficult balancing act given the freshness that Petit Courbu imparts rather than the more robust, exotic flavours of wines based on Gros Manseng. It does give some propensity to age, but don't wait long. Price £.

Passion de Charles Clément is a *moelleux* made from 100% Petit Manseng. It is aged in new oak and has the potential for fairly long aging. Price ££. A second sweet Pacherenc is more in the *doux* style; Tradition is a blend of 50% Petit Manseng and 50% Gros Manseng. It is also aged in new oak and careful handling is needed to prevent it overpowering the exotic fruit flavours. Price ££.

Tastings

L'Excellence de Marty 2006, Madiran.
80% Tannat, 10% Cabernet Franc, 10% Cabernet Sauvignon.
Deep garnet. Sweet, ripe black fruits with underlying red fruit and liquorice. On the Palette blackcurrants, prunes, raspberries and a spicy finish.
Very good, plenty of fruit, complex and soft.
July 2013

Domaine Laougué 2007, Madiran.
Tannat/Cabernet blend
Medium garnet. Creamy blackcurrant nose. Palette that is reminiscent of fireside smoke. Perhaps past its best as it lacks structure in the middle palette where one might expect the fruit to dominate. Still a nice spicy finish but drink soon.
February 2014

Passion de Charles Clément 2012, **Pacherenc sec.**
100% Petit Courbu.
Pale straw yellow, white peach, gooseberries with a mineral edge. Flavours of grapefruit and lime and a little vanilla oak. Lovely fresh style of dry Pacherenc. The oak is not intrusive and adds to the pleasure, excellent with fish. A second bottle will be stashed away for a year or so.
November 2013

Château Latreille-Sounac
Jean Marc Vanasten
32400 Riscle

Gers
Tel: +33 05 62 69 70 32
Email: Latreillesounac@orange.fr
Open: 9am to 12.30pm and 2pm to 8pm

Jean Marc has been a winemaker since 2002 with just six hectares of vines producing four different Madiran *cuvées*. **Château Latreille-Sounac, Cuvée Alexia, Cuvée Flavie** and **Cuvée 60.**

Domaines de Maouries
Philippe, Pascal and Isabelle Dufau
32400 Labarthète
Gers
Tel: +33 (0)5 62 69 63 84
Email: domainedemaouries@alsatis.net
Website: www.domainedemaouries.com
Open: Monday to Saturday 9am to 12.30pm and 2pm to 7pm.

Domaines de Maouries is one of the oldest *domaines* in the area, having been producing wine since 1907. The second generation of the Dufau family to run the affairs of the *domaine* split their duties, Pascal takes responsibility for the vineyards and the cellar and Isabelle deals with the account and direct sales and Philippe runs the commercial side of the business. Although officially retired André and Jacqueline are still to be found in the tasting room and ensuring that visitors see the *domaine* at its best.

The twenty eight hectares of vineyards are in the north of the *appellation* spread over twenty five plots enabling the production of Madiran, St Mont and Côtes de Gascogne wines. Generally south facing on excellent soils there is a concerted effort to ensure maximum ripeness by carrying out leaf and bud removal and green harvesting of excess bunches.

The family also open the *Chai* to groups for events where Pascal provides a range of gourmet dishes to accompany the wines. Not that it stops there; there is also a *gite* available to rent on the estate.

The Madirans are: **Orchis de Pyren** made from 100% Tannat. It receives eighteen months ageing in new oak. Vines are an average age of 40 years on clay limestone soils. This will improve for ten years or more. Price ££. **Cailloux de Pyren** is 95% Tannat and 5% Cabernet Sauvignon, twelve months aged in oak *barriques.* Give this as much time as the **Orchis**. Price £. **Couer de Pyren** is more in the *Tradition* style with 75% Tannat, 20% Cabernet Franc and 5% Cabernet Sauvignon. It is aged in barrels and in tanks. Drink after two or three years. Price £

Grains d'hiver is a Pacherenc *moelleux* made from 80% Petit Manseng and 20% Petit Courbu. Aged in oak *barriques*, 80% of which are new. This needs a bit of age to soften the oak but not so much that the fragrance of the Petit Courbu is lost. Price £

Also **Maori**, *Vin de Liqueur*. 100% Tannat. Price £

Domaine Monblanc
Daniel Saint Orens
32400 Maumusson-Laguian
Gers
Tel: +33 (0)5 62 69 82 51
Email: contact@domainemonblanc.fr
Website: wwwdomainemonblanc.fr

The Saint Orens family have run Domaine Monblanc since 1981. There are 6.5 hectares of vines, the Madiran vines are southwest facing on a clay limestone *terroir*, the Pacherenc vines are on southeast facing slopes with *grepp* soils. The family are committed to a minimum of artificial interventions in the vineyard. To assist with the ripening of grapes they do carry out a green harvest and use new and old oak in the ageing process.

The *Haut de Gamme* **Fût de Chêne** is a 100% Tannat *cuvée*. The wine is aged for twelve to fourteen months in oak *barriques*, 50% of which are new. This will age for five to ten years. Price £. The **Tradition** is made up of 60% Tannat and 40% Cabernet Franc. It is aged in tanks for eighteen months and will be ready to drink within 5 years. Price £

Domaine Monblanc is a *moelleux* made from 90% Petit Manseng and 10% Gros Manseng harvested after 11th November, aged for 6 months in new oak. This will age for five years +. Price £

Domaine du Moulié
Lucie and Michelle Charrier
32400 Cannet
Gers
Tel: +33 (0)5 62 69 77 75
Email: domainedumoulie@orange.fr
Website: www.domainedumoulie.com
Open: Monday to Saturday from 9am to 12pm and 2pm to 7pm.
Sunday: by appointment.

There are records of Domaine Moulié dating back to the mid-eighteenth century. At that time wines from Cannet were particularly sought after, their high reputation ensured a 10% premium compared to other wines in the area.

The first vintage produced by the Charrier family was the 1979, bottled in 1981. Prior to this the wines were sold *en vrac*, direct from tanks. Pierrette and Michel ran the *domaine* until 2002 when daughters Lucie and Michelle took over the reins. Since then the vineyard has moved to organic methods. The *domaine* has sixteen hectares, fourteen for Madiran and two for Pacherenc on clay soils on the east west ridge above the River Bergons.

Cuvée Chiffre is the *Haute de Gamme*, the **Tradition** is a blend of 75% Tannat, 20% Cabernet Franc, and 5% Cabernet Sauvignon/Fer Servadou. Cold pre-maceration takes four days and then maceration takes place over four weeks, aging is in tanks for twenty four months.

There is a Pacherenc Sec and a *Moelleux,* Cuvée L. Pouymene.

Tasting:

Cuvée Chiffre 2010, Madiran.
75% Tannat, 20% Cabernet Franc and 5% Cabernet Sauvignon.
Deep ruby, earthy with red fruits on the nose. Red fruits on the palette, tannins a little green. Perhaps a little time will help bring the wine together.
August 2013

Cru du Paradis
Jacques Maumus
65700 Saint Lanne
Hautes-Pyrénées
Tel: +33 (0)5 62 31 98 23
Email: cru.du.paradis@wanadoo.fr
Website: www.madirancruduparadis.com
Open: Monday to Friday from 8.30am to 8pm.
Saturday and Sunday: by appointment.

Cru du Paradis has twenty seven hectares of vines in Saint Lanne and Madiran and was founded in 1918. The vines are on clay soils facing south and southwest. Jacques has been responsible for a significant expansion of the *domaine* which only had eight hectares when he took over. There are four Madirans and three Pacherencs produced using various methods of vinification.

Reserve Royale, Vieille Vignes is 80% Tannat, 10% Cabernet Franc and 10% Cabernet Sauvignon. Maceration lasts for between fifteen and twenty one days. Ageing is for two years in oak *barriques*. **Tradition** and **Le Paradis des Pyrenées** are blends of 60% Tannat, 20% Cabernet Franc and 20% Cabernet Sauvignon. **Paradylys** is a modern style Madiran.

Cru du Paradis is the Pacherenc Sec, made of 30% Gros Manseng, Petit Manseng and Arrufiac and 10% *Petit* Courbu. The grapes are picked in early October and the ageing is in new oak *barriques* for three months. Tradition Pacherenc doux is made from 80% Gros Manseng *and* 20% Petit Manseng. The grapes are picked from the end of October to mid-November and ageing is in steel tanks for six months. This will age but will be fine drunk young. Reserve Royale is the Pacherenc *moelleux* made from Petit Manseng. The grapes are late harvested in December and the wine aged in oak *barriques* for eight months. There is the potential for this wine to age for five years +.

Tasting

Reserve Royale Vielle Vignes 2005, Madiran.
80% Tannat, 10% Cabernet Franc and 10% Cabernet Sauvignon.
Deep garnet. Complex nose of blackcurrant, cedar, red fruits and vanilla. Earthy blackcurrants on the palette, silky tannins and good length. Classic Madiran
July 2013

Château Peyros
Arnaud Lesgourges
64350 Corbiere-Albères
Pyrénées-Atlantiques
Tel: +33 (0)5 77 79 76 35
Email: contact@lesgourges.com
Website: www.vignobles-lesgourgues.com
Open: Monday to Friday by appointment.

Vines were to be found here as far back as the 17th century. The estate is the southern-most in the *appellation* and has been in the Lesgourges family since 1999. There are now twenty hectares of vines on silty clay soils, 70% of these are Tannat vines, 25% Cabernet Franc and 5% Cabernet Sauvignon.

The original cellar contains modern equipment, including stainless steel tanks and a micro-oxygenation system. However it would be wrong to think this was merely a hi-tech operation, the estate uses natural manure from its own sheep; some three hundred of them!

Château Peyros isn't the only estate owned under the banner of 'Vignobles Lesgourges'; the family own vineyards in other regions including another Tannat dominated estate in Uruguay, Domaine Monte de Luz. At Peyros Tannat covers half the vineyard with equal proportions of Cabernet Franc, Cabernet Sauvignon and Syrah making up the balance.

Greenwich .43N is made from 95% Tannat *and* 5% Cabernet Franc. Maceration takes for twenty five days with between twenty and twenty four months ageing in new French oak. The Tannat is from a single plot of two hectares with an average age over fifty years. Micro-oxygenation is used. Recommended ageing is for ten years plus. Price ££.

The **Vieille Vignes**, is 80% Tannat *with* 20% Cabernet Franc. Maceration takes twenty days and ageing is fourteen to twenty months in oak, of which 40% is new. The average age of the vines is between forty and fifty years. Micro-oxygenation is used. Age for 10 years. Price £.

The **Tradition** is made up of 60% Tannat and 40% Cabernet Franc. The wine, aged for twelve months; 50% in tank, 50% in oak is from vines aged between twenty and twenty years. Again micro-oxygenation used. This will age for up to five years but should be ready on release. Price £

Magenta (Tempo) is a 'wine bar' style made with 50% Tannat, and 50% Cabernet Franc. It is aged for twelve to eighteen in tanks. The grapes are taken from young vines. Drink young. Price £.

Tastings

Greenwich .43N 2001, Madiran.
95% Tannat, 5% Cabernet Franc.
Dark purple with aromas of pencil shavings, blackcurrant and raspberries.
On the palette blackcurrant and sour cherries, a touch of vegetal Cabernet Franc. Masculine style and probably will remain so, one for the purist. It needs fatty food to show its best.
May 2013

Vieille Vignes 2008, Madiran.
80% Tannat, 20% Cabernet Franc.
Dark garnet, pencil shavings, vanilla oak and a little red fruit. Flavours of liquorice and blackcurrant with a little spice. Good but should improve
June 2013

Tempo 2009, Madiran.
50% Tannat, 50% Cabernet Franc.
Medium purple, aromas of pencil shavings and red fruits. On the palette flavours of red fruits and cherries. Modern 'wine bar' Madiran. Almost like a

Loire red; Chinon or Bourgueil. Could almost be pure Cabernet Franc. Easy drinking.
May 2013

Château du Pouey
Bastien Lannusse
32400 Viella
Gers
Tel: +33 (0)5 62 69 78 25
Email: ch.pouey@orange.fr
Website: www.chateau-du-pouey.com

Bastien is the fourth generation of the Lannusse family to manage the estate and is regarded as a very good young winemaker. There are twenty two hectares of vines on the plateau; the stoney clay *terroir* produces powerful wines with good ageing potential. More fruity wines are produced on silty clay soils.

Bastien is a Madiran made from 100% *Tannat* aged for twelve months in oak *barriques*. It will age for ten years. **Reserve du Vigneron** is made from a blend of 85% Tannat and 15% Cabernet Franc/Cabernet Sauvignon. This will age for five to ten years. The **Tradition**, is 60% Tannat, 20% Cabernet Franc and 20% Cabernet Sauvignon. This is more suited to early drinking.

Lou Festayre is the Pacherenc Sec made from 80% Gros Manseng and 20% Petit Manseng. The grapes are picked mid-November and aged for six months in steel tanks. L'Aydasse, Pacherenc *moelleux* is 100% Petit Manseng picked from the end of November into December.

Tasting:

Tradition 2008, Madiran.
60% Tannat, 20% Cabernet Franc and 20% Cabernet Sauvignon.
Medium garnet. Blackcurrant on the nose. The palette has black and red fruits.
A good solid *Tradition*.
July 2013

Domaine Poujo
Famille Lannux
64330 Aydie
Pyrénées-Atlantiques
Tel: +33 (0)5 59 04 01 23

Email: domainepoujo@numero.fr
Open: Monday to Saturday from 9am to 12.30pm and 2pm to 7pm.
Sunday: by appointment.

The Lannux family have been in residence since 1970 however their first bottled vintage was 1981. There are ten hectares of vines, 50% of which are Tannat, with just under a third being for Pacherenc. The slopes are south and south-west and are gravelly clay soils with pebbles.

In 2000 Philippe took over from his father Claude, and since then new cellars and reception rooms have been built. Fermentation is carried out in steel tanks and ageing is in oak. Approximately a third of the oak is replaced each year.

There are two Madirans produced here are; **Fût de Chêne** is made from 95% Tannat and 5% Cabernet and aged in oak as the name suggests. The average age of the vines is twenty years. Keep for five years or so. Price ££. The **Tradition** is 80% Tannat *and* 20% Cabernet. Aged for sixteen months the wine should be ready to enjoy within a couple of years. Price £

The dry Pacherenc, Domaine Poujo is a blend of 50% Petit Manseng, 40% Gros Manseng and 10% Arrufiac. Made from twenty five year old vines the wine is best drunk young. The sweet Pacherenc, Domaine Poujo, is in the middle ground, made from 60% Gros Manseng and 40% Petit Manseng it is aged for ten months in tank to maintain its freshness. Both priced £.

Tasting:

Domaine Poujo 2011, **Pacherenc Sec**.
50% Petit Manseng, 40% Gros Manseng and 10% Arrufiac.
Pale straw yellow, Elderflowers and lemons on the nose. Exotic fruits and lemon on the palette. Fresh with lovely fruit. Good summer drinking.
August 2013

Domaine Sergent
Brigitte and Corinne Dousseau
32400 Maumusson-Laguian
Gers
Tel: +33 (0)5 62 69 74 93
Email: contact@domaine-sergent.com
Website: www.domaine-sergent.com
Open: Monday to Friday 8.30am to 12.30pm and 2pm to 6pm.
Sunday: by appointment

The *domaine* has been in the Dousseau family since 1902, the proprietor then was Herbert Dousseau, great grandfather to Brigitte and Corinne the current incumbents. The first estate bottling was in 1975.

There are 19.5 hectares of vines with an average age of approximately thirty five years, no artificial fertilizers are used. The estate makes use of micro-oxygenation and aging in both tanks and *barriques*.

Cuvée Élevage en Futs de Chêne is 100% Tannat aged in oak *barriques*. Micro-oxygenation is used. This will age for up to ten years. The **Tradition** is 70% Tannat, 20% Cabernet Franc and 10% Cabernet Sauvignon and is fermented in cement tanks. This wine should be ready within a couple of years.

Tradition is a Pacherenc doux made with a blend of 80% *Gros* and 20% *Petit Manseng* grapes picked in October. It is aged for six months and should be enjoyed young. Cuvée Élevé en Fûts de Chêne, is an oak aged Pacherenc Sec. Left *sur lies* for six months, Les Graines d'Église is a Pacherenc Moelleux which is cold stabilized and aged for seven months in oak *barriques*. This will stand a few years in the cellar. All the Pacherencs are priced £.

Tastings

Cuvée Élevage en Fûts de Chêne 2009, Madiran.
Deep ruby, pencil shavings and blackcurrant on the nose. Prunes and blackcurrants on the palette. Quite refined and well developed, could get even better.
November 2013

Élevé en Fûts de Chêne 2011, **Pacherenc Sec.**
Mid gold, aromas of exotic fruits the palette is exotic with quite a bit of oak evident. The Madiran is better in my opinion.
January 2014

Les Grains d'Église 2011, **Pacherenc Moelleux.**
Petit Manseng with a small amount of Gros Manseng.
Medium yellow with aromas of honeyed lemon. On the palette flavours of lemon and oranges. Pleasant and could improve with time.
July 2013

Domaine de Tailleurguet
François Bouby
32400 Maumusson-Laguian
Gers

Tel: +33 (0)5 62 69 73 92
Email: domaine.tailleurgeut@wanadoo.fr
Open: Monday to Saturday from 9am to 1pm and 2pm to 7pm.
Sunday: by appointment.

François took over the estate from his father-in-law and founder of the estate André Dartiques in 1990. André was one of the early advocates of Madiran wines and although retired retains his enthusiasm as a local historian and supporter of the work being done at the Domaine.

There are nine hectares of land under vines, two Madirans and a dry Pacherenc are produced. **Éleve en Fut** is an oak aged Madiran, the **Tradition,** made from 60% Tannat, 30% Cabernet Franc and 10% Cabernet Sauvignon is from vines aged on average thirty five years. Ageing is eighteen months *en cuvé*. This is fine to drink young.

The Pacherenc sec, Domaine de Tailleurguet is made from 40% Gros Manseng, 30% Arrufiac and 30% Petit Courbu. It is aged in oak *barriques* for six months. Drink early. All the wines here are priced £.

Tastings

Domaine de Tailleurguet 2009, Madiran.
Tannat/Cabernet blend.
Deep to dark ruby. Blackcurrants and liquorice on the nose, add to that some red fruit on the mid palette. Good solid *Tradition* style Madiran.
January 2014

Domaine de Tailleurguet 2009, **Pacherenc Sec.**
40% Gros Manseng, 30% Arrufiac and 30% Petit Courbu.
Pale yellow, aromas of gooseberry and apricot. Ripe apricot and pineapples on the palette. Gentle fruit, very fresh.
July 2013.

Domaine Bellegarde
M. Calderon
Tel: +33 (0)5 59 21 33 17

Domaine de Benguérets
Anne Marie Moutoue
65700 Madiran
Hautes-Pyrénées
Tel: +33 (0)5 62 96 33 55
Open: Monday to Sunday from 9am to 1pm and 2pm to 7pm.

Château de Diusse
64330 Diusse
Tel: +33 (0)5 62 96 33 55

Domaine Jourda
Laure Bournazel
65700 Soublecause
Hautes-Pyrénées
Tel: +33( )05 62 96 48 51(7)

Domaine Lacave
M Ponsolle
Tel: +33 (0)5 62 69 77 38

Domaine Lalanne
M. Capdevielle
Tel: +33 (0)5 62 69 74 65

Domaine Larroque
Raymond Galbardi
65700 Madiran
Hautes Pyrenees
Tel: +33 05 62 96 35 46

Domaine Mesté Bertrand
Monique Gaye
64350 Castillon
Pyrénées-Atlantiques
Tel: +33 (0)5 59 68 14 57

Open: Monday to Saturday from 9am to 12pm and 2pm to 7pm.

Domaine Peyrou
Jaques Brumont
32400 Viella
Gers
Tel: +33(0)5 62 69 90 12
Open: Monday to Saturday from 8.30am to 12.30pm and 2pm to 8pm.

Château de Piarrine
Patrick and Annie Achilli
32400 Cannet
Gers
Tel: +33 (0)5 62 69 77 66

La Vigne Du Moulin
Oliver Ledeveze
64330 Vialer
Pyrénées-Atlantiques
Tel:+33 (0)5 59 04 07 99

Bibliography

Madiran & Saint-Mont. Histoire et devenir des vignobles. Francis Brumont 1999

Vins du Sud-Ouest et des Pyrénées. Pierre Casamayor 1983

Madiran, le vin du terroir. Marie-Luce Cazamayou 2000

The Great Wines of France, France's Top Domaines and their Wines. Clive Coates MW 2005

The Wine Diet. Professor Roger Corder PhD MRPharmS **2009**

Le Vignoble du Madiran et Pacherenc du Vic-Bilh. André Dartigues et Stephane Granier 2001

The New France. A complete guide to contemporary French wine. Andrew Jefford 2006

Science, Vine and Wine in Modern France. Harry W. Paul 2002

South-West France. The Wines and Winemakers. Paul Strang 2009

Terroir. The role of Geology, Climate and Culture in the making of French Wines. James E. Wilson 1998

Wine Grapes. Jancis Robinson, Julia Harding and José Vouillamoz, 2012

Decanter Magazine.

La Revue du Vin de France.

www.vins-madiran.fr. ALTEMA-Generation Madiran

www.madiran-story.fr.

All photographs by David or Karen Perry

Map of Gascony (adapted) 09/13/2007 Wikipedia.fr Author- Larrousiney

Didier Barré *vigneron* at Domaine Berthoumieu bids farewell during the 2013 *vendange*.